Chapter 1: Introduction to Serial Killers
Defining Serial Killers

Serial killers have long fascinated and horrified society with their chilling acts of violence. In this subchapter, we delve into the intricate and complex world of these murderers, aiming to unravel the psychology behind their crimes. By examining their motives, patterns, and distinct characteristics, we gain a deeper understanding of the dark minds that perpetrate multiple murders over a period of time.

A serial killer can be defined as an individual who commits at least three murders with a cooling-off period in between each crime. This pattern differentiates them from mass murderers or spree killers, who typically kill multiple victims in a short period without any breaks. Serial killers are often driven by a compulsive need to kill, deriving pleasure or satisfaction from their heinous acts.

One of the distinguishing characteristics of serial killers is their ability to blend into society. They often lead seemingly ordinary lives, hiding their true nature behind a façade of normalcy. This ability to deceive and manipulate others is what allows them to continue their killing spree undetected for extended periods.

Motives behind serial killings can vary significantly, and understanding these motives is crucial to comprehend the psychology behind their crimes. Some serial killers are driven by a desire for power and control, deriving a sense of dominance from taking another person's life. Others may be motivated by sexual gratification, finding pleasure in the act of murder itself or in the subsequent mutilation of their victims. Additionally, there are those who commit serial murders due to a deep-rooted psychological disturbance, such as a desire for revenge or a need to justify their actions.

Examining the patterns of serial killers can provide valuable insights into their psychology. These murderers often exhibit a methodical approach, carefully selecting their victims and meticulously planning their crimes. They may follow a particular ritual or signature, leaving behind unique characteristics that distinguish their acts from random acts of violence. Understanding these patterns helps law enforcement in profiling and apprehending these criminals.

Historical Background

In order to truly understand the pIn conclusion, this subchapter delves into the chilling world of serial killers, exploring their psychology, motivations, and distinguishing characteristics. By unraveling the complexities of their minds, we gain a deeper understanding of the individuals who commit multiple murders over a period of time. This knowledge is not only essential for those interested in the crime genre but also for law enforcement agencies dedicated to preventing and solving these heinous crimes.

sychology behind serial killers, it is crucial to delve into the historical background that has shaped our understanding of these heinous crimes. Throughout history, there have been numerous instances of individuals who have committed multiple murders over a period of time, often exhibiting distinct characteristics or motives. Exploring the historical context of these crimes provides us with valuable insights into the twisted minds of these individuals.

One of the earliest recorded cases of a serial killer dates back to ancient Rome, with the infamous Emperor Nero. Nero was known for his sadistic tendencies, taking pleasure in torturing and killing both animals and humans. This historical figure serves as a chilling reminder that the roots of serial killing can be traced back centuries.

Moving forward in time, the 19th century witnessed the emergence of several notorious serial killers, such as Jack the Ripper. This unidentified killer terrorized the streets of London, brutally murdering and mutilating prostitutes. The case of Jack the Ripper remains unsolved to this day, captivating the imagination of crime enthusiasts and historians alike.

The 20th century witnessed a surge in serial killing cases, with names like Ted Bundy, Jeffrey Dahmer, and John Wayne Gacy becoming synonymous with evil. These individuals not only committed multiple murders but also exhibited distinct psychological patterns, often driven by sexual gratification, power, or a deep-rooted desire for control. Their crimes shocked the nation and forever etched their names in the annals of criminal history.

As the field of psychology advanced, so did our understanding of serial killers. Psychologists and forensic experts began to delve into the intricate workings of a serial killer's mind, attempting to unravel the motives and triggers behind their gruesome acts. This ongoing research has shed light on the psychological complexities that drive individuals to commit such heinous crimes.

By examining the historical background of serial killers, we gain a deeper understanding of the patterns and motivations that drive these individuals to commit multiple murders. From ancient Rome to modern-day cases, the chilling tales of these killers have left an indelible mark on society. Exploring their psychology allows us to better comprehend the factors contributing to their actions, ultimately leading us towards a more informed understanding of these complex and disturbing crimes.

Typologies of Serial Killers

Understanding the psychology and patterns of serial killers is a complex and intriguing subject. In this subchapter, we explore the typologies of serial killers, shedding light on the distinct characteristics and motives that drive these individuals to commit multiple murders over a period of time.

One of the most well-known typologies of serial killers is the Organized-Disorganized Dichotomy. This classification system focuses on the behavioral and psychological traits exhibited by these criminals. Organized serial killers are known for their meticulous planning, high intelligence, and ability to blend into society. They carefully select their victims, often targeting strangers, and leave little evidence behind. On the other hand, disorganized serial killers tend to be impulsive, disorganized in their crimes, and lack social skills. They often attack victims known to them and leave behind a chaotic crime scene.

Another typology is the Visionary Serial Killer, who believes they are compelled by a higher power, such as a deity or voices in their head, to commit murder. These individuals may suffer from severe mental illnesses, such as schizophrenia or psychosis, and often see their victims as symbolic representations of their delusions. The mission-oriented serial killer, in contrast, feels a deep sense of purpose in ridding the world of certain types of people they deem undesirable. They may target prostitutes, members of a particular race or religion, or individuals they perceive as morally corrupt.

Power and control play a significant role in the motivations of some serial killers. These individuals derive pleasure from exerting dominance and control over their victims. They may engage in sadistic acts, such as torture or sexual assault, to assert their authority and satisfy their desires. This typology, known as the Hedonistic Serial Killer, can further be divided into lust, thrill, and comfort subtypes, depending on the specific motivations driving their crimes.

While these typologies provide a framework for understanding serial killers, it is essential to acknowledge that some individuals may exhibit a mix of characteristics from different categories or may defy categorization altogether. The human mind is complex, and the motivations behind serial killings can vary greatly from case to case.

By studying the typologies of serial killers, we gain insight into the dark recesses of the human psyche. This knowledge allows us to better understand the patterns, motives, and psychological factors that contribute to these heinous crimes. Ultimately, unraveling the psychology behind serial killers is crucial for developing strategies to prevent future atrocities and ensure the safety of society.

Serial Killer Motivations

Understanding the motives behind the heinous crimes committed by serial killers is a perplexing and deeply disturbing endeavor. In this subchapter, we delve into the dark recesses of the human mind to unravel the psychology behind the actions of these individuals who commit multiple murders over a period of time, often with distinct characteristics or motives.

One of the most intriguing aspects of serial killers is the wide range of motivations that drive them to kill repeatedly. While each case is unique, certain patterns and underlying psychological factors have emerged through extensive research and analysis.

Some serial killers are driven by power and control. They derive a sick pleasure from exerting dominance over their victims, relishing in the fear and helplessness they inflict. Their crimes are meticulously planned, with a sadistic desire to manipulate and torment their prey. Power-seeking serial killers often exhibit charismatic personalities in their everyday lives, enabling them to lure unsuspecting victims into their clutches.

Another common motivation is the need for sexual gratification. These killers derive intense pleasure from the act of murder, often incorporating sexual rituals or acts in their crimes. Their victims become objects of lust, and the act of killing becomes intertwined with their twisted desires. This motivation is often accompanied by a deep-seated psychological disturbance, such as paraphilic disorders or sexual sadism.

Some serial killers are driven by a desire for fame or notoriety. They seek to leave a lasting mark on society, often taunting law enforcement or the media with cryptic messages or clues. These individuals are motivated by a narcissistic need for attention and recognition, relishing in the fear and fascination their crimes evoke in the public.

Furthermore, there are serial killers who are motivated by a combination of factors, making their crimes even more complex to unravel. Some may have experienced traumatic events or abuse in their past, leading to a deep-seated anger or desire for revenge. Others may suffer from severe mental illnesses, such as psychopathy or schizophrenia, which contribute to their lack of empathy and impulse control.

By understanding the motivations that drive serial killers, we gain valuable insights into their mindset and the patterns they exhibit. This knowledge allows law enforcement agencies and mental health professionals to develop more effective strategies for prevention, intervention, and profiling of potential offenders.

However, it is important to approach this topic with caution and empathy, as it deals with deeply disturbing and distressing subject matter. By shedding light on the psychology behind these crimes, we hope to contribute to a better understanding of the human mind while emphasizing the importance of early detection and intervention to prevent the devastating consequences of serial killers.

Chapter 2: The Making of a Serial Killer

Childhood Influences

The study of serial killers has long fascinated both the general public and experts in the field of criminology. What drives these individuals to commit multiple murders over a period of time, often with distinct characteristics or motives? To truly understand the psychology behind their crimes, it is crucial to examine the childhood influences that shape these individuals into the monsters they become.

Research has consistently shown that childhood experiences play a significant role in the development of a serial killer. Many notorious killers experienced a traumatic or abusive upbringing, marked by neglect, violence, or both. These early life experiences can have a profound impact on a child's emotional and psychological development, leading them down a dark and twisted path.

One common factor in the childhoods of serial killers is the presence of a dysfunctional family environment. This may include a lack of parental love and support, frequent arguments or violence between family members, or even the absence of one or both parents. Growing up in such an environment can leave a child feeling isolated, unloved, and emotionally scarred. As a result, they may develop a deep-seated anger, resentment, or desire for power and control, which can later manifest in their heinous crimes.

Another significant childhood influence on serial killers is the presence of early indicators of psychopathy or antisocial behavior. Many serial killers exhibit behavioral problems during their formative years, such as cruelty towards animals, fire-setting, or bedwetting beyond an appropriate age. These warning signs, if left unaddressed, can escalate into more violent and sadistic behaviors as they reach adulthood.

Moreover, some serial killers have been found to have a history of childhood abuse, whether physical, sexual, or emotional. This abuse can create a sense of shame, anger, and powerlessness that the individual may seek to exert control over by inflicting pain on others. The cycle of abuse they experienced becomes a vicious cycle perpetuated through their own violent actions.

Understanding these childhood influences is crucial for both prevention and detection. By identifying children who exhibit early signs of psychopathy or have experienced abuse, interventions can be implemented to address their emotional and psychological needs. Early intervention and support can potentially redirect these individuals away from a path of violence and towards a healthier future.

In conclusion, childhood influences play a significant role in shaping the minds of serial killers. A dysfunctional family environment, early indicators of psychopathy, and a history of abuse are common threads that can be traced back to their formative years. By unraveling the complex psychology behind these influences, experts can gain a deeper understanding of the motivations and patterns of these individuals, ultimately contributing to the prevention and detection of future acts of violence.

Early Warning Signs

Understanding the early warning signs of a potential serial killer is crucial for society to identify and prevent these heinous crimes. In this subchapter, we delve into the intricate psychology behind the actions of these individuals, examining the patterns and characteristics that often accompany their murderous tendencies. By unraveling the psychology behind the crimes, we hope to shed light on the dark corners of the human mind and contribute to the prevention of future atrocities.

Serial killers are not born overnight; their development follows a twisted trajectory that can be traced back to early warning signs. One of the most common indicators is a history of cruelty towards animals during childhood. Many notorious serial killers, such as Jeffrey Dahmer and Ted Bundy, exhibited a fascination with torturing and killing animals at a young age. This behavior often serves as a precursor to the violence they later inflict upon fellow humans.

Another early warning sign is a troubled childhood, characterized by neglect, abuse, or witnessing violence. The absence of a stable and nurturing environment can contribute to the growth of violent tendencies. Serial killers may experience feelings of powerlessness, rejection, or humiliation during their formative years, which can fuel their desire for control and dominance over others.

Additionally, a predisposition to antisocial behavior is often evident in the early stages of a serial killer's life. They may display a lack of empathy, an inability to form meaningful relationships, and a disregard for societal norms. These individuals often have difficulty conforming to rules and authority, leading to a sense of rebellion and a propensity for violent acts.

As the warning signs progress, it becomes vital to recognize the specific personality traits commonly associated with serial killers. They often exhibit manipulative and charming behaviors, allowing them to easily gain the trust of their victims. This deceptive charm masks their true intentions, making it even more challenging to detect their sinister motives.

By examining the early warning signs, patterns, and psychological traits of serial killers, we aim to empower individuals to identify potential threats in their communities. Knowledge of these indicators can prompt early intervention and preventive measures, potentially saving countless lives. It is our responsibility as a society to be vigilant and proactive in recognizing and addressing the complex psychological makeup of those who may become serial killers. Through understanding and education, we can hope to create a safer world.

Family Dynamics

In order to truly understand the complex psychology behind the crimes committed by serial killers, it is essential to delve into the intricate web of their family dynamics. The environment in which a person grows up plays a significant role in shaping their character, beliefs, and behavioral patterns. Serial killers are no exception to this rule, often displaying patterns that can be traced back to their formative years.

Family dynamics refer to the interactions, relationships, and power structures within a family unit. It encompasses factors such as parental influence, sibling relationships, family structure, and the overall emotional climate at home. These dynamics can have a profound impact on an individual's development, including their propensity towards violence and criminal behavior.

Numerous studies have identified common themes in the family backgrounds of serial killers. Many perpetrators of these heinous crimes have experienced dysfunctional family dynamics, characterized by abuse, neglect, or a lack of emotional support. Physical, sexual, or psychological abuse can profoundly affect a child's psyche, often leading to feelings of anger, powerlessness, and a distorted sense of reality. These negative experiences can fuel a deep-seated resentment towards others and result in violent tendencies later in life.

Moreover, the absence of positive role models or stable familial relationships can also contribute to the development of a serial killer. In some cases, serial killers may have grown up without a father figure or experienced strained relationships with their parents or siblings. This lack of guidance and support can lead to feelings of isolation, low self-esteem, and a desperate search for control and dominance.

Understanding the family dynamics of serial killers is crucial for law enforcement and psychologists to identify potential warning signs and intervene early on. By recognizing the impact of dysfunctional family environments, professionals can work towards implementing preventive measures and providing necessary support to at-risk individuals.

It is important to note that not all individuals who come from troubled family backgrounds become serial killers. However, studying family dynamics helps shed light on the complex interplay between nature and nurture, providing valuable insights into the psychological and behavioral patterns of these notorious criminals.

In conclusion, family dynamics play a significant role in shaping the psychology of serial killers. The dysfunctional environments in which they grew up can contribute to the development of violent tendencies and a distorted sense of reality. By understanding these dynamics, professionals can better identify and intervene with individuals at risk, potentially preventing future tragedies.

Childhood Trauma

In the dark and twisted realm of serial killers, the origins of their heinous acts often lie hidden within the depths of their childhood trauma. Understanding the profound impact of early experiences is crucial to unraveling the psychology behind these chilling crimes. This subchapter delves into the complex relationship between childhood trauma and the emergence of a serial killer, shedding light on the patterns and motives that drive these individuals to commit multiple murders over an extended period.

Childhood trauma can manifest in various forms, such as physical, sexual, or emotional abuse, neglect, or witnessing violent acts. These traumatic events often shape a disturbed and distorted perspective on the world, leading to a fractured psyche that seeks control and power through acts of violence. Serial killers frequently harbor deep-seated feelings of anger, resentment, and a burning desire for revenge, which are rooted in their traumatic past.

The subchapter explores the correlation between specific types of childhood trauma and the distinct characteristics exhibited by serial killers. It examines how abuse, for instance, can foster a sense of powerlessness and perpetuate a cycle of violence, fueling their need for dominance and control over their victims. Additionally, neglect during formative years can result in emotional detachment, a lack of empathy, and a propensity for sadistic acts.

Moreover, the subchapter delves into the long-term psychological effects of childhood trauma on the development of a serial killer's personality. It explores how trauma can disrupt the normal psychological growth of an individual, leading to maladaptive coping mechanisms, such as dissociation or the creation of alternate personalities. These coping strategies enable the killer to compartmentalize their actions, allowing them to operate undetected for extended periods.

By understanding the intricate interplay between childhood trauma and the emergence of serial killers, this subchapter aims to shed light on the underlying psychological factors that drive these individuals to commit repeated acts of violence. It seeks to provide a deeper comprehension of the motivations, patterns, and distinct characteristics exhibited by serial killers, helping criminologists, psychologists, and law enforcement agencies to better identify, apprehend, and prevent such heinous crimes.

Inside the Mind of a Serial Killer: Unraveling the Psychology Behind the Crimes is an essential resource for those fascinated by the intricate workings of the criminal mind. Examining the psychology and patterns of individuals who commit multiple murders over a period of time, this book offers a comprehensive exploration of the dark recesses of the human psyche that give rise to these chilling killers.

Psychological Factors

Understanding the mind of a serial killer requires delving into the complex web of psychological factors that contribute to their heinous actions. These individuals, who commit multiple murders over a period of time, often exhibit distinct characteristics and motives that set them apart from other criminals. By unraveling the psychology behind their crimes, we can gain valuable insights into the motivations, thought processes, and patterns of behavior that drive these individuals to commit such heinous acts.

One of the key psychological factors associated with serial killers is their propensity for psychopathy. Psychopathy is a personality disorder characterized by a lack of empathy, remorse, and a disregard for the rights and feelings of others. Serial killers often display a high level of psychopathy, enabling them to detach themselves emotionally from their victims, viewing them merely as objects to satisfy their dark desires.

Another important psychological factor is the presence of childhood trauma or abuse. Many serial killers have experienced a traumatic childhood, which can contribute to the development of violent tendencies. These individuals may have suffered from neglect, physical or sexual abuse, or witnessed violence within their families. Such experiences can shape their perception of the world, leading to a distorted view of relationships, power, and control.

Moreover, the need for dominance and control is a recurring theme in the psychology of serial killers. These individuals often seek to exert power over their victims, deriving a sadistic pleasure from the manipulation and domination of others. This desire for control extends beyond the act of killing, as many serial killers engage in post-mortem rituals or keep mementos to maintain a sense of power and control over their victims even after their death.

Furthermore, the concept of fantasy plays a vital role in the psychology of serial killers. Many offenders create elaborate and vivid fantasy worlds that serve as an outlet for their darkest desires. These fantasies often involve themes of domination, violence, and sexual gratification. The act of killing becomes a means to fulfill these fantasies, blurring the line between reality and the twisted world inside their minds.

Understanding the psychological factors that drive serial killers is crucial for law enforcement and criminal profilers. By recognizing the patterns, motivations, and triggers associated with these individuals, authorities can develop effective strategies for prevention, identification, and apprehension. Moreover, a deeper understanding of these psychological factors can help society identify potential warning signs and intervene before someone becomes a victim.

In conclusion, the subchapter on psychological factors provides a comprehensive exploration of the intricate aspects that contribute to the mind of a serial killer. By examining the role of psychopathy, childhood trauma, the need for dominance and control, and the influence of fantasy, we can gain valuable insights into the psychology behind these heinous crimes. By unraveling these psychological factors, we aim to shed light on the motivations and patterns of behavior exhibited by serial killers, ultimately contributing to a better understanding of this dark and disturbing phenomenon.

Psychopathy and Antisocial Personality Disorder

Psychopathy and Antisocial Personality Disorder: Unraveling the Dark Minds of Serial Killers

Serial killers have long been a subject of fascination for crime enthusiasts, psychologists, and the general public alike. Their heinous crimes, committed over an extended period, often leave communities in fear and law enforcement agencies tirelessly searching for answers. To truly understand these individuals and the motives behind their actions, it is crucial to delve into the complex world of psychopathy and antisocial personality disorder.

Psychopathy is a personality disorder characterized by a lack of empathy, shallow emotions, and an inclination towards manipulative and impulsive behavior. It is essential to note that not all psychopaths become serial killers, but many serial killers exhibit psychopathic traits. Their ability to detach from the consequences of their actions and their lack of remorse make them particularly dangerous individuals.

Antisocial Personality Disorder (ASPD), on the other hand, is a broader term that encompasses individuals who consistently disregard the rights of others, engage in criminal behavior, and show a blatant disregard for societal norms. Many serial killers meet the criteria for ASPD, but not all individuals with ASPD become murderers.

The combination of psychopathy and ASPD creates a deadly concoction within the minds of serial killers. These individuals often possess a set of distinct characteristics and motives that set them apart from other criminals.

One of the key distinguishing features of serial killers is their need for power and control. They derive immense pleasure from dominating their victims, exerting complete control over their lives, and ultimately snuffing out their existence. This desire for dominance is rooted in the psychopathic traits of grandiosity and sadism.

Serial killers also exhibit a pattern of repetitive behavior, whereby they meticulously plan and execute their crimes. This repetition is often driven by a psychological need to relive the experience, as the initial thrill subsides with each subsequent killing. This compulsion to replicate the act suggests a deep-rooted psychological disturbance that is prevalent in these individuals.

While the motives behind serial killings can vary, many killers seek notoriety and a sense of power through their crimes. They may be motivated by a desire for fame, a need to feel superior, or an attempt to gain control over their own lives by exerting control over others.

In conclusion, delving into the minds of serial killers requires an understanding of psychopathy and antisocial personality disorder. These disorders, when combined, create a volatile combination that drives individuals to commit multiple murders. By examining their distinct characteristics and motives, we can begin to unravel the psychology behind their heinous crimes and gain valuable insights into the dark minds of these individuals.

Narcissism and Egotism

Narcissism and Egotism: Understanding the Dark Traits that Drive Serial Killers

In the twisted and chilling realm of serial killers, it is essential to delve into the depths of their minds to comprehend the psychology behind their heinous crimes. Among the various psychological traits that emerge from this exploration, narcissism and egotism stand out as prominent factors driving their actions. These dark and destructive characteristics provide valuable insights into the motivations and patterns of these individuals who commit multiple murders over an extended period.

Narcissism, at its core, is an excessive self-love and an inflated sense of superiority. Serial killers often possess an insatiable need for admiration and validation, feeding off the fear and attention their crimes generate. Their delusions of grandeur and entitlement fuel their desire to exert power and control over others, making them feel invincible. This narcissistic personality trait leads them to commit atrocious acts, seeking validation for their twisted superiority complex.

Egotism, on the other hand, centers around an excessive and exaggerated sense of self-importance. Serial killers often believe they are untouchable, above the law, and even beyond the reach of moral boundaries. Their inflated egos compel them to view their victims as mere objects, dehumanizing them and justifying their acts as necessary for their own gratification. This psychopathic trait enables them to commit multiple murders without remorse or empathy.

Understanding the interplay between narcissism and egotism provides crucial insights into the distinct characteristics and motives of serial killers. Their insatiable thirst for power, coupled with their belief in their own superiority, drives them to seek out victims who they perceive as weaker or inferior. They meticulously plan their crimes, relishing in the control and dominance they exert over their victims. The psychological thrill derived from this power dynamic becomes addictive, leading to a repetitive pattern of killings.

Furthermore, these dark traits also contribute to the development of a signature style or modus operandi, which can be identified by investigators. The narcissistic need for recognition often leads serial killers to leave behind specific calling cards or symbols at crime scenes, marking their territory and taunting law enforcement agencies. Their egotistical desire to outsmart authorities compels them to engage in a dangerous cat-and-mouse game, relishing in the attention they receive.

In conclusion, the study of narcissism and egotism is crucial in unraveling the psychology behind serial killers. These traits offer profound insights into their motivations, patterns, and signature behaviors. Understanding the dark minds of these individuals is essential for law enforcement agencies, criminal profilers, and society as a whole, as it enables us to identify, apprehend, and prevent future acts of unspeakable evil.

Sadism and Power Dynamics

In the dark and twisted world of serial killers, one disturbing aspect that often comes into play is the intricate relationship between sadism and power dynamics. Exploring this unsettling connection can shed light on the psychology behind these heinous crimes, providing valuable insights into the minds of these cold-blooded murderers.

Sadism, commonly defined as deriving pleasure from inflicting pain, is a key component in understanding the motives and actions of many serial killers. It is within the context of sadism that power dynamics emerge as a driving force behind their crimes. These killers possess an insatiable thirst for power and control, which they seek to exercise over their victims in the most sadistic and brutal ways imaginable.

The power dynamics at play in the mind of a serial killer are complex and multifaceted. These individuals often have deep-rooted feelings of inferiority and powerlessness, which they compensate for by exerting dominance over others. By subjecting their victims to unspeakable acts of violence and degradation, they derive a sense of power and control that temporarily alleviates their own feelings of inadequacy.

Furthermore, the power dynamics extend beyond the act of killing itself. Serial killers often engage in a twisted game of cat and mouse with law enforcement and society as a whole. They relish the power they hold over the authorities who desperately try to apprehend them, leaving behind tantalizing clues and messages to assert their superiority. This power dynamic fuels their egos, providing them with a sadistic thrill that only intensifies their thirst for control.

Understanding the interplay between sadism and power dynamics is crucial for profiling and apprehending serial killers. By comprehending the motivations and psychological patterns underlying their crimes, law enforcement can develop strategies to prevent future acts of violence and protect potential victims. Additionally, studying these dynamics can help mental health professionals identify early warning signs and intervene before individuals escalate into becoming serial killers.

In conclusion, the exploration of sadism and power dynamics within the context of serial killers provides a chilling glimpse into the depths of human depravity. By unraveling the psychology behind these crimes, we gain valuable insights into the motives and patterns of these individuals. This knowledge is essential for the field of criminology, as it aids in the prevention, apprehension, and understanding of these terrifying and enigmatic individuals.

Chapter 3: The Dark Fantasies
Understanding the Role of Fantasies

In the dark and intricate world of serial killers, the role of fantasies cannot be underestimated. These twisted and often gruesome imaginings play a crucial part in the psychology behind the heinous crimes committed by these individuals. To truly comprehend the mind of a serial killer, we must delve deep into the inner workings of their fantasies.

Fantasies, in the context of serial killers, refer to vivid and elaborate mental images that these individuals construct in their minds. These fantasies serve as a catalyst, fueling their desire to commit acts of violence and murder. They provide an escape from reality, allowing the killer to embark on a journey of power, control, and sadistic pleasure.

The psychology behind these fantasies is multifaceted. For some serial killers, their fantasies act as a coping mechanism, a way to deal with past trauma or feelings of powerlessness. By indulging in these twisted daydreams, they regain a sense of control and dominance over others, temporarily relieving their internal turmoil.

Furthermore, fantasies can serve as a form of rehearsal for the actual acts of violence. Serial killers meticulously plan and prepare for their crimes, often replaying their fantasies in their minds over and over again. This mental rehearsal allows them to hone their techniques, refine their strategies, and ultimately carry out their murderous intentions with chilling precision.

It is important to note that not all individuals who fantasize about violence become serial killers. Fantasies alone do not determine criminal behavior. However, for those who do cross the line, their fantasies gradually evolve and intensify, becoming an integral part of their daily lives. The boundaries between fantasy and reality blur, leading them down a path of no return.

Understanding the role of fantasies in the minds of serial killers is crucial for law enforcement, psychologists, and society as a whole. By unraveling the intricate psychology behind these dark imaginings, we can gain valuable insights into the motives, patterns, and characteristics of these individuals. Ultimately, this knowledge can assist in the identification, apprehension, and prevention of future serial killers. By recognizing the signs and understanding the psychological factors at play, we can work towards a safer society, where the depths of these violent fantasies are not brought to life.

Escalation of Fantasies

In the dark and twisted world of serial killers, the escalation of fantasies is a crucial aspect that unravels the psychology behind their heinous crimes. It is within these fantasies that the seeds of destruction are sown, slowly transforming seemingly ordinary individuals into cold-blooded murderers. This subchapter delves into the chilling progression of these fantasies, shedding light on the patterns and motivations that drive serial killers to commit multiple murders over time.

To understand the escalation of fantasies, one must first comprehend the intricate web of a serial killer's mind. These individuals possess a unique psychological makeup, often harboring deep-rooted traumas, disturbed childhoods, or an overwhelming desire for power and control. As they succumb to their dark desires, their fantasies become increasingly vivid, evolving from simple thoughts to elaborate scenarios that fuel their murderous tendencies.

The escalation of fantasies can be traced back to the early stages of a serial killer's life. They may start with harmless daydreams or fantasies of power and control, which gradually intensify over time. As their fantasies become more elaborate, the killers begin to experience a distorted sense of reality, blurring the line between their imagination and the real world. This psychological transformation is a pivotal turning point that propels them into the realm of actual violence.

Distinct characteristics and motives often emerge in the escalation of these fantasies. Some serial killers are driven by a need for dominance, seeking to exert control over their victims. Others may be motivated by a twisted desire for sexual gratification, deriving pleasure from the pain and suffering they inflict. Understanding these distinct characteristics and motives is crucial in profiling and apprehending these criminals before they can claim more innocent lives.

By examining the escalation of fantasies, we gain valuable insights into the minds of serial killers. It allows us to decipher the patterns and triggers that lead to their brutal acts, enabling law enforcement agencies and psychological professionals to develop effective strategies for prevention and intervention.

In "Inside the Mind of a Serial Killer: Unraveling the Psychology Behind the Crimes," we take a dark and unsettling journey into the psyche of these monstrous individuals. Through extensive research and analysis, we explore the progression of their fantasies, shedding light on the twisted motivations that drive them to commit multiple murders.

This subchapter aims to satisfy the curiosity of crime enthusiasts and those fascinated by the psychology of serial killers. By examining the escalation of fantasies, we hope to shed light on this disturbing aspect of their crimes, ultimately contributing to our collective understanding of the chilling world of serial killers.

Role of Media and Popular Culture

The role of media and popular culture in shaping public perception and understanding of serial killers cannot be underestimated. In recent decades, the fascination with these enigmatic criminals has reached unprecedented levels, thanks in large part to the media's relentless coverage and our society's insatiable appetite for true crime stories. This subchapter explores the profound impact of media and popular culture on our understanding of serial killers, shedding light on the psychology and patterns behind their heinous crimes.

Media outlets, whether traditional or digital, have become key players in disseminating information about serial killers. They provide a platform for experts, investigators, and survivors to share their insights and experiences. By analyzing the psychology and patterns of these individuals who commit multiple murders over time, media coverage helps uncover the motivations and characteristics that drive these criminals to commit such horrific acts. In doing so, it allows us to gain a deeper understanding of the psychology behind serial killing.

Popular culture, including books, movies, and television shows, also play a significant role in shaping public perception of serial killers. These mediums often depict the chilling and twisted minds of these criminals, captivating audiences with their narratives. While some argue that popular culture glamorizes or even sensationalizes serial killers, it cannot be denied that it also serves as a vehicle for educating the public about their behavior and the importance of understanding the psychological factors that contribute to their crimes.

However, it is crucial to recognize the potential dangers of media and popular culture's influence on our perception of serial killers. The intense focus on these criminals can sometimes overshadow the victims and their families, leading to the perpetuation of a cult-like fascination that glorifies their actions. Care must be taken to ensure that media coverage and popular culture representation strike a balance between satisfying our curiosity and respecting the dignity of those affected by these crimes.

In conclusion, the role of media and popular culture in examining the psychology and patterns of serial killers is undeniable. Through their coverage and representation, they provide a platform for understanding the complexities of these criminals and the motives behind their actions. However, it is essential to approach this subject matter with sensitivity and responsibility to avoid glamorizing or sensationalizing their crimes. By doing so, we can better educate the public about the psychology of serial killers and work towards preventing such atrocities in the future.

Fantasies as a Catalyst for Murder

In the dark and twisted world of serial killers, fantasies play a chilling role as catalysts for their heinous crimes. These disturbed individuals harbor deep-rooted desires and elaborate daydreams that eventually manifest into a brutal reality. Understanding the psychology behind these fantasies is crucial in unraveling the complex minds of serial killers.

The human mind possesses an astonishing ability to conjure up vivid and disturbing fantasies; however, for most individuals, these remain confined within the realms of imagination. But for the select few who become serial killers, these fantasies turn into an obsession, fueling their murderous intent and setting them on a path of destruction.

One common characteristic shared by many serial killers is the need for control. Their fantasies often revolve around the power they believe they possess over their victims' lives. Through their sadistic daydreams, they envision themselves dominating, torturing, and ultimately ending the lives of others. These fantasies provide them with a sense of empowerment, which they are unable to achieve in their everyday lives.

Moreover, the fantasies of serial killers serve as an escape from reality. They create an alternate world where their darkest desires are not only acceptable but also glorified. In this twisted realm, their victims become mere pawns in a macabre game, fulfilling their twisted yearnings for dominance and control.

Interestingly, fantasies can also act as a rehearsal for serial killers. They meticulously plan and visualize their crimes, refining their techniques and perfecting their methods. These rehearsals, often played out countless times in their minds, provide them with a sense of confidence, enabling them to carry out their gruesome acts with precision and detachment.

Examining the role of fantasies in the psychology of serial killers sheds light on the disturbing patterns that emerge. It allows us to delve into the depths of their disturbed minds and comprehend the motivations behind their actions. By understanding these fantasies, we gain valuable insight into the intricate web of emotions, desires, and impulses that drive these individuals to commit multiple murders.

In conclusion, the fantasies of serial killers serve as a potent catalyst for their murderous acts. These dark daydreams provide them with a sense of control, an escape from reality, and act as rehearsals for their heinous crimes. Unraveling the psychology behind these fantasies is crucial in comprehending the twisted minds of serial killers and uncovering the patterns and motives that drive them.

Chapter 4: Serial Killers and Their Victims

Victim Selection Process

Understanding the victim selection process is crucial in unraveling the psychology behind serial killers' heinous crimes. These individuals carefully choose their targets, often with distinct characteristics or motives in mind. By exploring the intricacies of their victim selection process, we gain invaluable insights into the twisted minds of these murderers.

Serial killers are meticulous planners, spending considerable time and effort identifying potential victims. Their selection process is driven by a combination of factors, including their psychological needs, fantasies, and specific characteristics they seek in their victims.

One significant aspect of the victim selection process is the killer's motive. Some may target individuals who remind them of a specific person from their past, seeking vengeance or attempting to recreate an earlier traumatic experience. Others may be driven by a need for power or control, selecting victims who appear vulnerable or submissive. Understanding these underlying motives can shed light on the reasons behind their crimes.

Serial killers often exhibit a pattern in their victim selection, which helps police investigators create profiles and predict their next moves. The patterns may revolve around age, gender, appearance, or even occupation. These patterns can provide invaluable clues, aiding law enforcement in their pursuit of justice.

Furthermore, the victim selection process is influenced by the killer's psychological fantasies. These fantasies can be sexually or sadistically driven, and the victims are chosen to fulfill these dark desires. By examining these fantasies, we gain a glimpse into the twisted inner world of the killer and the disturbing thoughts that fuel their actions.

It is important to note that serial killers often target victims who they perceive as "lesser" or less likely to be missed by society. They may prey on marginalized individuals, such as sex workers or transient populations, believing that their crimes will go unnoticed or garner less attention from law enforcement.

By delving into the victim selection process, we gain a deeper understanding of the complexities surrounding serial killers. Exploring their motives, patterns, and psychological fantasies allows us to comprehend the depths of their disturbed minds. This knowledge is crucial for law enforcement in identifying and apprehending these individuals, as well as for individuals interested in studying the psychology of these chilling crimes.

Vulnerability Factors

When it comes to understanding the mind of a serial killer, exploring the various vulnerability factors that contribute to their development is crucial. These factors are like puzzle pieces that, when combined, paint a picture of how these individuals evolve into the monsters we fear.

One of the most significant vulnerability factors is childhood trauma. Many serial killers have experienced abuse, neglect, or witnessed violence during their formative years. These traumatic experiences can shape their perception of the world and distort their sense of empathy and morality. The lack of a nurturing environment can lead to a deep-seated anger and a desire for power and control, which often manifests in their heinous crimes.

Another vulnerability factor is a dysfunctional family dynamic. Serial killers often come from broken homes, where parental figures may be absent, abusive, or struggle with substance abuse. This unstable environment can contribute to a lack of emotional support and healthy socialization, leaving these individuals feeling isolated and disconnected from society. This isolation can further fuel their desire for dominance and the need to assert control over others.

Psychological disorders and personality traits also play a significant role in vulnerability factors. Many serial killers exhibit psychopathic or sociopathic tendencies, such as a lack of remorse, shallow emotions, and an inability to form meaningful relationships. These individuals often have an intense need for stimulation and may engage in thrill-seeking behavior, which can escalate into acts of violence.

Furthermore, the presence of paraphilias, such as sadism or necrophilia, can contribute to the vulnerability of becoming a serial killer. These deviant sexual fantasies and behaviors can create a dangerous mix when combined with other vulnerability factors, pushing individuals to act on their darkest impulses.

While vulnerability factors provide insight into the development of a serial killer, it is essential to understand that not everyone with a traumatic past or psychological disorder becomes a murderer. The combination of these factors, along with external triggers, such as a significant life event or exposure to violent media, can set the stage for the emergence of a serial killer.

By examining these vulnerability factors, we can begin to unravel the psychology behind the crimes committed by serial killers. This knowledge is vital in identifying potential warning signs and developing effective preventive measures to protect society from the horrors that these individuals can inflict. It is through understanding the intricacies of their minds that we can hope to dismantle the patterns and motives of these deeply disturbed individuals.

Victim Profiling

Subchapter: Victim Profiling

Understanding the mind of a serial killer is a complex endeavor, with victim profiling being a crucial aspect of unraveling the twisted psychology behind their crimes. Profiling allows law enforcement and forensic psychologists to gain insight into the motives, patterns, and characteristics of these individuals who commit multiple murders over an extended period of time.

Serial killers often select their victims based on specific criteria that align with their psychological needs and fantasies. By analyzing the victims' traits, investigators can uncover valuable information about the killer's preferences, methods, and potential vulnerabilities.

One of the primary factors in victim selection is vulnerability. Serial killers tend to target individuals who are more likely to be in vulnerable positions, such as sex workers, runaways, or individuals with a history of substance abuse. These victims are often marginalized in society, making them easier targets for the killer's violent fantasies. By recognizing this pattern, law enforcement can focus on protecting those who are at higher risk.

Another important aspect of victim profiling is identifying the killer's signature. A signature is a unique behavior or ritual that a serial killer incorporates into their crimes, which may not be necessary to accomplish the act but is driven by their psychological motivations. For example, a killer might consistently leave a specific object at the crime scene or pose the victims in a particular manner. By understanding these signatures, investigators can link seemingly unrelated murders and establish patterns that lead to the identification and capture of the killer.

Moreover, victim profiling can shed light on the killer's motives and psychology. Some serial killers are driven by power and control, while others may be motivated by sexual gratification or revenge. By examining the characteristics of the victims and the manner in which they were targeted and killed, investigators can gain insights into the killer's underlying psychological state.

In conclusion, victim profiling plays a crucial role in understanding the psychology and patterns of serial killers. It helps investigators identify vulnerable individuals who may be targeted, uncover the killer's signature, and gain insights into their motives and psychological makeup. By delving into the mind of a serial killer through victim profiling, law enforcement and forensic psychologists can bring justice to the victims and prevent future tragedies.

Victimology Patterns

Understanding the patterns and characteristics of victims in serial killings is a crucial aspect of unraveling the psychology behind these heinous crimes. In this subchapter, we delve deep into the world of victimology, shedding light on the intriguing connections and recurring themes that emerge when examining the individuals targeted by serial killers.

One of the most striking aspects of victimology patterns is the selection process employed by these murderers. Serial killers often have distinct preferences when it comes to their victims, which can vary based on factors such as age, gender, occupation, or physical appearance. By analyzing these patterns, we gain valuable insights into the mindsets and motivations of these criminals.

Age is a common distinguishing factor in victimology patterns. Some serial killers specifically target vulnerable individuals, such as children or the elderly, who may be easier to overpower or control. Others may prefer victims within a specific age range, either due to personal fantasies or traumatic experiences from their own past. Understanding these age-related preferences is crucial in developing strategies to protect potential victims and apprehend these dangerous offenders.

Gender is another key aspect of victimology patterns. Numerous serial killers exhibit a preference for either males or females, often driven by deep-rooted psychological issues or unresolved conflicts related to gender dynamics. This gender-specific selection can also be motivated by the killer's desire for power, control, or sexual gratification. Recognizing these gender-related patterns is vital in identifying potential victims and developing effective prevention measures.

Moreover, certain professions or lifestyles may make individuals more susceptible to becoming victims of serial killers. Sex workers, hitchhikers, or individuals with transient lifestyles are often targeted due to their increased vulnerability and the perception that their disappearances may go unnoticed. By studying these victimology patterns, law enforcement agencies and society can work together to provide better protection and support for those at higher risk.

By unraveling the victimology patterns in serial killings, we gain a deeper understanding of the psychology behind these crimes. This knowledge empowers law enforcement agencies to develop more effective profiling techniques, investigate cases more efficiently, and ultimately prevent future tragedies. Furthermore, it enables us to provide support and resources to potential victims, ultimately creating a safer society for all.

Types of Victims

One of the most chilling aspects of studying the mind of a serial killer is understanding the different types of victims they target. Serial killers are individuals who commit multiple murders over a period of time, often with distinct characteristics or motives. Their choice of victims is not random, but rather a reflection of their psychological makeup and underlying motives. In this subchapter, we will delve into the various types of victims that serial killers tend to target, shedding light on the twisted psychology behind their crimes.

1. Vulnerable Individuals:

Serial killers often prey on vulnerable individuals who are less likely to receive attention from law enforcement or media. These victims may include sex workers, runaways, or individuals living on the fringes of society. The killers may perceive these individuals as easy targets, believing that their absence will go unnoticed or be dismissed by society.

2. Marginalized Groups:

Serial killers frequently target marginalized groups such as ethnic minorities, the homeless, or individuals with mental health issues. These victims may already face societal prejudice and discrimination, making them more vulnerable to exploitation and violence. The killers may exploit the biases and prejudices of society to carry out their crimes, knowing that their victims' disappearances may attract less attention.

3. Power and Dominance Seekers:

Some serial killers derive pleasure and satisfaction from exerting power and dominance over their victims. They may target individuals who possess qualities they envy or wish to control, such as beauty, intelligence, or success. These killers derive a sense of power and superiority from overpowering and controlling their victims, often engaging in sadistic acts to maintain their dominance.

4. Specific Demographics:

Certain serial killers focus on specific demographics such as young children, teenagers, or women. These killers may have unresolved psychological issues related to their own childhood experiences or a deep-seated hatred towards a particular gender or age group. They may see their victims as representative of a larger group and seek to vent their frustrations or enact revenge.

5. Opportunistic Targets:

While some serial killers meticulously choose their victims, others act impulsively, seizing any opportunity that presents itself. These killers may strike when they come across someone who fits their general victim profile, regardless of specific characteristics. Opportunistic serial killers may choose victims based on convenience, proximity, or the circumstances they find themselves in at a given moment.

Understanding the types of victims targeted by serial killers is crucial in unraveling the psychology behind their crimes. By recognizing the patterns and motives behind their victim selection, law enforcement and criminal profilers can develop strategies to prevent future tragedies and bring these individuals to justice. However, it is essential to remember that the victims of these heinous crimes deserve our utmost empathy and respect, as we strive to shed light on the dark corners of the mind of a serial killer.

Geographic Profiling

Geographic Profiling: Unmasking the Hidden Patterns of Serial Killers

One of the most intriguing aspects of studying serial killers is the analysis of their geographic patterns. Geographic profiling, a method that combines psychology, criminology, and geography, allows investigators to uncover hidden links and patterns within a killer's crime scenes. By examining the geographic aspects of a series of murders, experts gain valuable insights into the offender's behavior, motives, and even their potential location.

The study of geographic profiling emerged as a powerful tool in the late 20th century, spearheaded by the brilliant minds of criminologists and psychologists. Through meticulous analysis of crime scenes, investigators discovered that serial killers often operate within a defined geographic area known as their "comfort zone." This region typically encompasses the offender's home, workplace, or other familiar locations. By focusing on this zone, investigators can narrow down their search for the killer, potentially saving lives and bringing justice to the victims' families.

Understanding the geographic patterns of a serial killer can provide crucial information about their psychology and motives. For example, some offenders may choose victims who live or work in a particular area, reflecting a personal grudge or vendetta against a specific neighborhood or community. Others may select victims from different locations, indicating a more random or opportunistic approach. By examining the spatial relationships between crime scenes, investigators gain valuable insights into the killer's mindset, helping them build a psychological profile that may eventually lead to their identification.

The analysis of geographic patterns also sheds light on a killer's modus operandi, or their preferred method of operation. By examining the similarities between crime scenes, investigators can identify patterns such as the type of victims targeted, the time of day the crimes were committed, or even the specific locations chosen. This knowledge aids in creating a comprehensive profile of the killer, allowing law enforcement to anticipate their next move and potentially prevent further tragedies.

Geographic profiling has proven to be an invaluable tool in solving numerous serial murder cases. By combining the psychological and geographical aspects of a killer's behavior, investigators have successfully tracked down and apprehended some of the most notorious offenders in history. This subchapter will delve deep into the world of geographic profiling, exploring real-life case studies, the techniques employed by investigators, and the groundbreaking contributions that this field has made to the understanding of serial killers.

Whether you are a true crime enthusiast or a professional in the field, this subchapter promises to unravel the fascinating psychology behind the crimes committed by serial killers. Prepare to be captivated as we uncover the hidden patterns and geographical secrets that lie inside the minds of these notorious individuals.

Chapter 5: Signature and MO

Defining Signature and MO

Defining Signature and MO: Unraveling the Psychology Behind Serial Killers' Crimes

In the dark and twisted world of serial killers, a chilling phenomenon emerges - the signature and modus operandi (MO). These two concepts are crucial in understanding the psychology and patterns behind the heinous crimes committed by these individuals. As we delve into the minds of these killers, we uncover the intricate details that set them apart and provide valuable insights into their motives and characteristics.

Signature refers to the unique and personal touch that a serial killer leaves behind at each crime scene. It is like an artist's signature on a masterpiece, a distinct calling card that they cannot resist leaving. This signature can manifest in various ways, from the choice of victims to the specific manner in which they are killed. It represents the killer's individuality and personal satisfaction, often reflecting deep-rooted psychological needs or fantasies.

On the other hand, the modus operandi (MO) refers to the practical aspects of the killer's method. It encompasses the specific techniques, rituals, and procedures employed during the commission of their crimes. The MO can include aspects such as the selection of victims, the type of weapon used, the location of the crime scene, and even the disposal of the bodies. Unlike the signature, the MO is adaptable and subject to change as the killer evolves and refines their strategies.

Understanding the interplay between signature and MO is essential in profiling and apprehending serial killers. By analyzing the consistent elements of their crimes, investigators can begin to unravel the complex psychological makeup of these individuals. The signature often serves as a psychological fingerprint, revealing underlying motivations, fantasies, and obsessions. In contrast, the MO provides clues about the killer's level of organization, planning skills, and level of control over their victims.

It is important to note that the signature and MO can evolve and change over time, as the killer becomes more experienced or seeks new ways to satisfy their twisted desires. This evolution can provide investigators with invaluable insights into the killer's psychological development and potentially aid in their capture.

The study of signature and MO not only assists law enforcement in solving crimes but also sheds light on the motivations and psychological underpinnings of serial killers. By examining these distinct characteristics and patterns, we gain a deeper understanding of the complexities of their minds, allowing us to better protect society from their malevolent actions.

In conclusion, the concepts of signature and MO are crucial in unraveling the psychology behind the crimes of serial killers. These distinct characteristics and patterns provide valuable insights into their motives, fantasies, and level of control. By dissecting the signature and MO, we strive to understand the minds of these individuals, ultimately helping to prevent future atrocities and bring justice to the victims.

The Importance of Signature

In the dark and twisted world of serial killers, one element often emerges as a chilling trademark of their crimes - the signature. A signature is a unique and distinct behavior, motive, or characteristic that sets a particular serial killer apart from others. It is a calling card left behind at the crime scene, not only to taunt law enforcement but also to satisfy the twisted desires of the killer themselves. Understanding the importance of a signature is crucial in unraveling the psychology behind these heinous crimes.

For those fascinated by the minds of serial killers, examining their signatures provides valuable insights into their motives, fantasies, and psychological makeup. By analyzing the patterns and consistencies in a killer's signature, investigators can gain a deeper understanding of their mindset, allowing them to profile the killer and potentially predict their future actions.

Some signatures may be overt and obvious, such as specific mutilation or staging of the victims' bodies. Others, however, can be more subtle, like the use of a specific weapon, a particular method of disposal, or the selection of victims with similar physical attributes. These unique elements become the killer's personal trademark, distinguishing their crimes from others and fueling their twisted satisfaction.

Moreover, understanding the importance of a signature is not limited to law enforcement. The knowledge of signatures can also aid forensic psychologists, criminologists, and other professionals in their quest to comprehend the inner workings of the criminal mind. By delving into the motives behind a signature, researchers can gain valuable insights into the psychological factors that drive these individuals to commit such heinous acts repeatedly.

Furthermore, the importance of signatures extends beyond the realm of understanding and profiling serial killers. It plays a vital role in solving cold cases, linking seemingly unrelated crimes, and identifying potential copycat killers. Identifying a signature can help investigators establish a common thread among multiple crimes, leading to the identification and capture of the perpetrator.

In conclusion, the importance of a signature in the world of serial killers cannot be overstated. It serves as a window into the dark recesses of their minds, providing crucial insights into their motives, fantasies, and psychological makeup. By understanding and analyzing a killer's signature, investigators, researchers, and professionals can unlock the secrets behind their crimes, potentially preventing future tragedies and bringing justice to the victims and their families.

Evolution of Signature

In the dark and twisted world of serial killers, one aspect that has fascinated both criminologists and the general public alike is the evolution of their signature. The signature refers to the unique and distinguishing characteristics or motives that a serial killer develops over time. Understanding this evolution is crucial in unraveling the psychology behind their heinous crimes.

At the outset, it is important to differentiate between a signature and a modus operandi (MO). While the MO refers to the method or technique employed by a killer to commit their crimes, the signature encompasses the distinctive aspects that are not necessary for the crime to be completed successfully. These aspects often serve as a psychological need or gratification for the killer, making it a vital area of study.

The evolution of a serial killer's signature can be a gradual process that evolves with each murder committed. Initially, they may exhibit a lack of a consistent pattern, making it difficult for investigators to link the crimes. However, as they continue their murderous spree, a pattern begins to emerge. This pattern can include a specific choice of victims, a particular manner of killing, or even a trademark ritual performed before or after the act.

The signature evolves as the killer gains confidence and becomes more comfortable in their actions. It becomes a personal stamp that distinguishes them from other criminals and gives them a sense of power and control. The signature can also serve as a way for the killer to relive their crimes, providing them with a psychological thrill or satisfaction.

In some cases, the signature may escalate and become more elaborate or violent over time. This escalation often reflects the killer's desire for increased notoriety or the need to intensify their emotional gratification. It may also indicate a progression in their psychological pathology or a desire to challenge law enforcement.

Understanding the evolution of a signature is crucial for investigators profiling a serial killer. By analyzing the distinct characteristics and motives, investigators can gain insights into the killer's psychology, which can aid in their identification and capture. Additionally, it helps establish patterns and connections between seemingly unrelated crimes, ultimately leading to a greater understanding of the serial killer phenomenon.

In conclusion, the evolution of a serial killer's signature is a fascinating and crucial aspect to examine when delving into the psychology behind these heinous crimes. The unique characteristics and motives that develop over time provide a window into the killer's mindset, shedding light on their psychological needs and motivations. By understanding this evolution, investigators can better profile and apprehend these dangerous individuals, bringing justice to their victims and closure to the communities affected by their actions.

Modus Operandi: Execution of the Crime

As we delve into the twisted psyche of a serial killer, it becomes imperative to understand the intricate details of their modus operandi - the method and pattern by which they execute their heinous crimes. The execution of a crime is a chilling glimpse into the mind of these individuals, revealing their motives, tactics, and distinct characteristics that set them apart from other criminals.

One of the most intriguing aspects of a serial killer's modus operandi is their ability to carefully select and stalk their victims. Unlike other criminals who may act impulsively, serial killers often meticulously plan their attacks, choosing their targets based on specific characteristics or motives. This selection process may be driven by a variety of factors, such as personal fantasies, a desire for power or control, or even a need to enact revenge. By studying their victims and understanding their motives, we gain valuable insights into the twisted workings of a killer's mind.

Once a target has been chosen, a serial killer will typically employ a range of tactics to gain access to their victim. These tactics may include creating a false sense of trust, exploiting vulnerabilities, or using a disguise to blend into their surroundings. By mastering the art of manipulation and deception, they are able to lure their victims into a vulnerable state, where they can then carry out their sinister intentions.

The actual act of committing murder is often marked by distinctive patterns and rituals unique to each killer. These patterns can provide crucial clues for investigators, helping them to link multiple crimes together and identify the work of a serial killer. From the choice of weapon to the method of disposal, every detail meticulously planned and executed by the killer leaves a signature of their twisted personality behind.

Understanding the modus operandi of a serial killer is not only essential for law enforcement but also for society as a whole. By examining their methods, we can develop strategies and preventative measures to identify and apprehend these dangerous individuals before they claim more innocent lives. Moreover, it gives us a glimpse into the dark corners of human psychology, forcing us to confront the terrifying reality that exists within the minds of these killers.

In the study of serial killers, the examination of their modus operandi is a crucial component. It allows us to unravel the psychology behind their crimes and gain a deeper understanding of their motives, patterns, and distinct characteristics. Through this knowledge, we strive to protect ourselves and create a safer society, while still grappling with the unsettling truth that exists within the darkest recesses of the human mind.

Chapter 6: Murderous Patterns and Rituals

Ritualistic Behaviors

In the eerie realm of serial killers, where darkness and depravity intertwine, one chilling aspect often emerges: ritualistic behaviors. These peculiar patterns shed light on the twisted psychology behind the crimes, providing insight into the minds of these heinous individuals. This subchapter delves into the enigmatic world of ritualistic behaviors, unraveling their significance and exploring their presence in the realm of serial killers.

Serial killers, by definition, are individuals who commit multiple murders over a period of time, often with distinct characteristics or motives. Within this subset of criminals, ritualistic behaviors frequently emerge as a means of exerting control, satisfying inner desires, or as a reflection of their disturbed psyche. These behaviors manifest in various ways, creating a macabre tapestry of rituals that both intrigue and horrify.

One common ritualistic behavior among serial killers is the meticulous staging of crime scenes. These murderers meticulously arrange their victims' bodies, leaving behind eerie tableaus that serve as a twisted form of self-expression. From arranging bodies in specific poses to positioning objects with calculated precision, these killers seek to leave their mark on the scene, asserting their dominance over life and death.

Another ritualistic behavior prevalent among serial killers is the collecting of souvenirs. These macabre tokens serve as mementos of their gruesome acts, allowing them to relive the thrill long after the crime has been committed. From locks of hair to personal belongings, these souvenirs hold a sinister significance, acting as trophies that validate their twisted desires.

Furthermore, certain serial killers engage in ritualistic acts before, during, or after their murders. These acts may involve dressing up in specific attire, adopting personas, or adhering to a strict routine. Such rituals provide a sense of structure and familiarity, enabling these individuals to enter a dark mindset and carry out their heinous acts with a disturbing sense of purpose.

The presence of ritualistic behaviors in the realm of serial killers is a perplexing phenomenon that continues to captivate the minds of criminologists and psychologists alike. By examining these behaviors, experts hope to unravel the complex motivations and psychological underpinnings that drive these individuals to commit such horrific acts.

As we delve deeper into the psychology of serial killers, it becomes apparent that ritualistic behaviors serve as both a manifestation of their disturbed psyche and a means of asserting control over their victims and the crime itself. By studying these behaviors, we inch closer to understanding the twisted minds behind the crimes, bringing us one step closer to unraveling the psychology of these elusive and chilling individuals.

Rituals as Control Mechanisms

In the twisted world of serial killers, rituals play a significant role in their heinous acts. These individuals who commit multiple murders over a period of time often develop distinct patterns and motives, which are deeply rooted in their psychology. This subchapter delves into the dark and perplexing realm of rituals as control mechanisms, shedding light on the motivations and behaviors of these infamous criminals.

Serial killers, driven by their insatiable desires and compulsions, often establish rituals to exert control over their victims and surroundings. These rituals serve as a means to maintain a sense of power and dominance, providing a twisted sense of order in their chaotic lives. By adhering to these rituals, they create a semblance of control over their actions and the outcome of their crimes.

One common aspect of these rituals is the carefully planned and executed modus operandi. Serial killers meticulously plan their murders, following specific steps and sequences. This methodical approach gives them a sense of control, allowing them to predict and manipulate the outcome of their crimes. The repetition of these rituals reinforces their belief in their own superiority and invincibility.

Furthermore, rituals serve as a psychological coping mechanism for these disturbed individuals. The act of repeating specific actions or behaviors provides them with a sense of comfort and familiarity, masking the underlying anxiety and turmoil within. These rituals create a sense of detachment, allowing them to distance themselves emotionally from the gruesome acts they commit.

Additionally, rituals can also act as a form of communication or expression for serial killers. They may leave behind a signature or a distinctive mark at the crime scene, symbolizing their control and leaving a chilling message for investigators. These signatures often become their calling card, allowing them to assert their dominance and instill fear in both the authorities and the public.

Understanding the significance of rituals in the minds of serial killers is crucial for law enforcement and forensic psychologists. By unraveling the psychology behind these rituals, investigators can gain valuable insights into the motives, patterns, and potential future actions of these criminals. This knowledge can aid in profiling, apprehending, and preventing similar crimes in the future.

In conclusion, rituals act as control mechanisms for serial killers, allowing them to exert power, establish order, and cope with their inner turmoil.

These dark and twisted rituals provide insights into the complex psychology of these individuals, shedding light on the motives, patterns, and behaviors that drive their heinous crimes. By exploring and comprehending these rituals, we can hope to better understand, prevent, and bring justice to the victims of these chilling predators.

Patterns in Killing Methods

Understanding the patterns in killing methods is essential when examining the psychology of serial killers. These individuals, driven by distinct characteristics or motives, commit multiple murders over a period of time. By unraveling the psychology behind their crimes, we gain valuable insights into the minds of these criminals.

One of the most striking patterns observed among serial killers is the choice of killing method. While each killer has their own unique approach, certain commonalities emerge. These patterns shed light on the psychological factors that drive these individuals to commit heinous crimes.

Firstly, many serial killers favor specific killing methods that provide them with a sense of control and power. Strangulation, for instance, allows the killer to physically dominate their victims, exerting complete control over their lives. This method gives them a sense of power and dominance, fulfilling their psychological needs.

Another prominent pattern is the use of weapons, such as knives or firearms. For some killers, these tools serve as extensions of their own aggression and violence. The act of stabbing or shooting their victims provides a visceral outlet for their deep-seated anger and rage. The choice of weapon often reflects the killer's desire for a personal connection with their victims, as they witness the immediate consequences of their actions.

Additionally, some serial killers employ methods of poisoning or suffocation. These methods are often preferred by individuals who seek to exert a more covert form of control. By manipulating their victims' environment or food, these killers can carry out their crimes without direct confrontation, evading suspicion and prolonging their killing spree.

Furthermore, certain serial killers engage in sexually motivated crimes, using methods such as rape or torture. These individuals derive pleasure from the sadistic control they exert over their victims, often escalating their violence to satisfy their twisted desires. The combination of sexual gratification

and violence forms a disturbing pattern in the psychology of these killers. Understanding these patterns in killing methods is crucial for profiling and apprehending serial killers. By recognizing the motives behind their choice of methods, law enforcement can better anticipate and prevent future crimes. Moreover, psychologists can delve deeper into the psychological aspects of these individuals, offering insights into their twisted minds.
In conclusion, patterns in killing methods provide valuable insights into the psychology of serial killers. The choice of method reflects their need for control, power, and violence, as well as their sadistic or sexually motivated tendencies. By unraveling these patterns, we gain a better understanding of the minds behind these heinous crimes, aiding in the prevention and detection of future offenders.

Rituals and Symbolism

When studying the twisted minds of serial killers, it becomes evident that their crimes are not merely acts of violence but rather carefully orchestrated rituals filled with symbolism. These rituals and symbols provide crucial insights into the psychology and patterns of these individuals who commit multiple murders over a period of time, often with distinct characteristics or motives.

Serial killers are known for their need to exert control and power over their victims, and rituals serve as a means to achieve this dominance. These rituals can manifest in various forms, such as specific patterns of killing, staging of the crime scene, or even the choice of weapons. By meticulously following these rituals, serial killers create a sense of familiarity and mastery, which helps them satisfy their psychological cravings.

Symbolism also plays a significant role in the twisted minds of these murderers. Serial killers often assign symbolic meanings to their actions, victims, or even the locations where they commit their crimes. These symbols can vary from highly personal associations to more universal archetypes. For example, a killer may consistently target victims who remind them of a past traumatic experience or embody qualities they despise. By doing so, they are enacting their own distorted narrative and attempting to gain a sense of power or redemption.

Understanding these rituals and symbols is crucial for criminal profilers and investigators. By analyzing the patterns and symbols associated with a specific killer, they can gain insights into their motives, psychological state, and even predict their next moves. Identifying these rituals and symbols can also be instrumental in linking different crime scenes or connecting seemingly unrelated murders to a single perpetrator, aiding in the ultimate apprehension of the killer.

However, it is important to approach the study of rituals and symbolism with caution. Serial killers are unique individuals, each with their own intricacies and motivations. Therefore, generalizations must be made with care, as not all killers exhibit the same patterns or symbolism. Nonetheless, delving into the world of rituals and symbolism allows us to unravel the complex psychology behind these heinous crimes, shedding light on the dark recesses of the human mind.

In conclusion, rituals and symbolism are integral components in the psychology of serial killers. These twisted individuals use rituals to exert control and power over their victims, while symbols provide them with a sense of purpose and meaning. By deciphering these rituals and symbols, investigators can gain valuable insights into the motives and psychological state of these criminals, aiding in their capture and understanding of their heinous acts. The exploration of rituals and symbolism opens a window into the mind of a serial killer, allowing us to better comprehend the depths of human depravity.

Chapter 7: The Psychology Behind the Crimes Power and Control

In the dark and twisted world of serial killers, one prevailing theme that consistently emerges is the insatiable desire for power and control. These individuals, driven by their sinister urges, embark on a path of destruction, leaving behind a trail of victims and a chilling legacy that haunts society to its core. Understanding the psychology behind their crimes is key to unraveling the complexities of these disturbed minds.

Serial killers are not merely driven by a compulsion to kill, but rather by a desperate need to exert dominance and control over their victims. By taking the lives of others, they gain a sense of power that they lack in their own lives. It is this power that becomes intoxicating, fueling their desire to continue their murderous spree.

The quest for control is manifested in the meticulous planning and execution of their crimes. Serial killers often exhibit a high level of intelligence, carefully selecting their victims and methodically eluding law enforcement. By maintaining control over their actions, they believe they can manipulate the world around them, asserting their dominance over both the living and the dead.

Patterns begin to emerge when examining the psychology of serial killers. Many exhibit a need for control in all aspects of their lives, often stemming from feelings of inadequacy or powerlessness. The ability to dictate the fate of their victims gives them a sense of superiority and satisfaction that temporarily alleviates their internal turmoil.

Motives behind these heinous acts can vary, but the underlying need for power and control remains constant. Some killers seek revenge, targeting individuals whom they perceive as having wronged them. Others may be driven by a sadistic desire to inflict pain and suffering upon others, deriving pleasure from the fear they instill in their victims.

As we delve into the minds of these monsters, it becomes evident that understanding their psychology is crucial in preventing future tragedies. By studying the patterns, motivations, and triggers of serial killers, law enforcement can develop more effective profiling techniques, ultimately bringing these criminals to justice before they can claim more innocent lives.

In conclusion, the subchapter "Power and Control" sheds light on the dark motivations that drive serial killers to commit their heinous acts. The need for power and control becomes a dominant force in their lives, leading them down a path of destruction and despair. By unraveling the psychology behind their crimes, we gain a deeper understanding of the twisted minds that haunt our society and can work towards preventing future tragedies caused by these deranged individuals.

Gratification and Sadism

In the dark and twisted world of serial killers, the motivations behind their heinous acts are often complex and deeply rooted in their psychological makeup. One of the most disturbing aspects of their behavior is the gratification they derive from committing these gruesome crimes. This subchapter delves into the twisted psychology of serial killers, exploring the link between gratification and sadism, and shedding light on the disturbing patterns that emerge.

For many serial killers, the act of taking a life is not merely an impulse, but a carefully orchestrated event that brings them immense pleasure. These individuals often exhibit sadistic tendencies, deriving pleasure from inflicting pain and suffering on their victims. It is through this sadistic gratification

that they fuel their insatiable desire to kill again and again.
The roots of this sadistic behavior can often be traced back to their childhood experiences. Many serial killers have a history of abuse, neglect, or trauma, which has warped their sense of empathy and morality. Their sadistic tendencies may be a way for them to regain a sense of power and control, as they seek to inflict the same pain they once endured upon others.
In addition to the gratification gained from causing suffering, serial killers often develop a ritualistic pattern to their crimes. These rituals can range from specific methods of killing to the disposal of the victim's bodies. The repetition of these rituals provides a sense of structure and control for the killer, further enhancing their gratification. It is through these patterns that investigators can begin to unravel the psychology behind their crimes and potentially identify common characteristics or motives.

Understanding the connection between gratification and sadism is crucial in the investigation and prevention of serial killings. By identifying individuals who exhibit sadistic tendencies and understanding the underlying factors that drive their behavior, law enforcement agencies can potentially intervene before they escalate to becoming serial killers.

This subchapter serves as a chilling reminder of the dark recesses of the human mind and the lengths some individuals will go to satisfy their sadistic desires. It highlights the importance of studying the psychology of serial killers, as it provides valuable insights into their motives and patterns. By unraveling the psychology behind their crimes, we can work towards a better understanding of these individuals and take steps to prevent future atrocities.

Need for Recognition and Fame

Title: Need for Recognition and Fame: Unveiling the Dark Desires of Serial Killers

Introduction:

Within the twisted labyrinth of a serial killer's mind lies a deep-rooted need for recognition and fame. This subchapter explores the psychological underpinnings behind this disturbing phenomenon, illuminating the motivations that drive individuals to commit multiple murders over extended periods. Delving into the psyche of serial killers, we aim to shed light on the patterns, characteristics, and motives that define this chilling niche of criminal behavior.

The Quest for Infamy:

Serial killers often possess an insatiable thirst for recognition, seeking to etch their names into the annals of history. Their crimes are meticulously planned and executed, with calculated precision, aimed at gaining notoriety and leaving an indelible mark on society. The desire for fame becomes a twisted obsession, fueling their escalating acts of violence.

Psychological Perspectives:

From a psychological standpoint, the need for recognition and fame in serial killers can be rooted in various factors. Some killers suffer from deep-seated feelings of insignificance or neglect, and their crimes serve as a desperate attempt to assert their existence and importance. Others may harbor narcissistic tendencies, craving the adulation and attention that accompanies their gruesome deeds. The twisted desire for fame can also stem from a desire for power and control over others, as their actions grant them a sense of superiority and dominance.

The Media's Role:

The media plays a pivotal role in satisfying the craving for recognition that serial killers yearn for. Sensationalistic coverage of their crimes amplifies their notoriety, often turning them into household names and transforming their horrific acts into a form of twisted celebrity. Serial killers revel in the attention bestowed upon them, which further fuels their ego and motivates them to continue their killing spree.

Distinct Characteristics and Patterns:

Examining the psychology of serial killers reveals common patterns and characteristics amongst this deviant group. Many exhibit a desire to outwit law enforcement and leave behind a trail of breadcrumbs, challenging investigators to catch them. Some killers even engage in taunting behaviors, such as sending cryptic messages or leaving behind trophies, further cementing their infamy.

Conclusion:

The need for recognition and fame is a disturbing facet of the psychology behind serial killers. Unraveling the motivations that drive these individuals to commit heinous crimes is essential in understanding their mindset and preventing future tragedies. By shedding light on this dark aspect of their psyche, we hope to contribute to a deeper understanding of the complexities surrounding serial killers, ultimately aiding in the development of strategies to combat this chilling phenomenon.

Exploration of Dominance and Violence

In the morbid realm of serial killers, the exploration of dominance and violence is a crucial aspect that sheds light on the twisted psychology behind their heinous crimes. Understanding the motivations, patterns, and characteristics of these individuals is essential to unraveling the complex web of their disturbed minds.

Serial killers, by definition, are individuals who commit multiple murders over a period of time, often with distinct characteristics or motives. Their actions are driven by a desire for dominance, control, and the infliction of fear upon their victims. This subchapter delves deep into the dark recesses of their minds, attempting to glean insights into what compels these killers to commit such gruesome acts.

One of the central themes surrounding serial killers is their need for dominance. Through violence, they seek to establish power and control over others, often deriving a sick satisfaction from the suffering they cause. This subchapter explores the underlying psychological factors that contribute to this insatiable thirst for dominance, examining theories such as childhood trauma, personality disorders, and psychopathy.

Furthermore, the exploration of violence in the context of serial killers uncovers patterns and distinct characteristics that may help in identifying and apprehending these dangerous individuals. By dissecting their methods, motives, and the aftermath of their crimes, we can gain valuable insights into their modus operandi. This subchapter delves into the varying degrees of violence exhibited by different types of serial killers, ranging from organized and methodical to disorganized and impulsive.

Moreover, the exploration of dominance and violence in the context of serial killers also delves into the psychological aftermath of their crimes. Understanding the effects of their actions on both the victims and society at large is crucial in preventing and combating such atrocities. This subchapter examines the lasting impact of serial killer violence, discussing the trauma experienced by survivors, the ripple effect on communities, and the efforts of law enforcement to bring these killers to justice.

In summary, this subchapter, "Exploration of Dominance and Violence," delves into the disturbing psychology behind serial killers. By examining their motivations, patterns, and characteristics, we gain a deeper understanding of their twisted minds. This exploration is essential for the audience of "crime" and the niche of "Serial killers: Examines the psychology and patterns of individuals who commit multiple murders over a period of time, often with distinct characteristics or motives."

Chapter 8: Serial Killers and Society

Media Influence and Public Fascination

In the realm of true crime, few subjects captivate the public's imagination more than serial killers. These individuals, driven by their dark desires, commit multiple murders over an extended period, often leaving behind a trail of fear, confusion, and devastation. The media plays a significant role in shaping public perception and fascination with these heinous crimes, both for better and for worse.

The media has a profound influence on our understanding and interpretation of serial killers. Through news reports, documentaries, books, and movies, the public gains access to the disturbing details of these crimes. This exposure, however, can have detrimental effects. Sensationalized portrayals in the media often focus on the gruesome aspects of the crimes, glorifying the killers and their actions. This can inadvertently fuel the public's fascination, transforming these criminals into cult-like figures and even inspiring copycat behavior.

Furthermore, the media's portrayal of serial killers can perpetuate harmful stereotypes and misconceptions. They are often depicted as deranged, monstrous individuals without any redeeming qualities. While it is crucial to acknowledge the enormity of their crimes, it is equally important to delve deeper into the psychological factors driving their behavior. By understanding the complex motivations, childhood traumas, and mental illnesses that contribute to their actions, we can gain valuable insights into preventing and addressing such atrocities.

Despite these potential pitfalls, the media also has the power to educate and raise awareness about the psychology and patterns of serial killers. Responsible reporting can shed light on the factors that lead to these crimes, such as early warning signs, common traits, and societal influences. By examining case studies and expert analysis, the public can better comprehend the complexities surrounding these individuals and the impact of their crimes on victims and society at large.

Ultimately, the media's influence on the public's fascination with serial killers is a double-edged sword. It is essential for consumers of crime content, particularly those interested in the psychology and patterns of serial killers, to approach these narratives critically and responsibly. By seeking out accurate, well-researched information from reputable sources, we can satisfy our curiosity while respecting the gravity of the subject matter.

"Inside the Mind of a Serial Killer: Unraveling the Psychology Behind the Crimes" aims to explore the intricate relationship between media influence and public fascination with these criminals. By delving into case studies, expert opinions, and the societal implications of these crimes, this book seeks to provide a comprehensive understanding of serial killers and their psychological makeup. It is an invitation for the crime niche and serial killer enthusiasts to delve deeper, challenge preconceived notions, and engage in a thoughtful exploration of this dark and perplexing subject matter.

Serial Killers as Cultural Icons

Serial killers have long been subjects of fascination within popular culture. From books and movies to documentaries and podcasts, the morbid curiosity surrounding these individuals has only grown over time. This subchapter delves into the intriguing concept of serial killers as cultural icons, exploring the reasons behind society's obsession with these dark figures.

One possible explanation for our captivation with serial killers is the psychological aspect. The human mind is inherently curious, especially when it comes to understanding what drives individuals to commit heinous crimes. By examining the psychology and patterns of these killers, we hope to shed light on their motives and uncover a deeper understanding of the human psyche.

Furthermore, serial killers often possess distinct characteristics that set them apart from other criminals. Some may have specific modus operandi or signatures, while others display peculiar behavioral traits. These unique aspects of their crimes make them intriguing subjects for study and analysis, captivating the minds of crime enthusiasts and professionals alike.

Additionally, the media plays a significant role in the cultural elevation of serial killers. True crime documentaries, movies, and books have gained massive popularity in recent years, feeding the public's fascination with these notorious criminals. Serial killers have become pop culture icons, with their names and stories known by millions worldwide. They have become an integral part of our collective consciousness, a dark fascination that captivates audiences across the globe.

However, it is essential to acknowledge the ethical implications of portraying serial killers as cultural icons. While their stories may entertain and educate, it is crucial to remember that the victims and their families suffer immense pain and loss. By glamorizing these killers, we risk glorifying their actions and perpetuating a cycle of violence.

In conclusion, serial killers have become cultural icons due to our innate curiosity about the human mind and our desire to understand the motivations behind their crimes. The distinct characteristics and patterns displayed by these individuals make them captivating subjects for study. However, we must approach this fascination with caution and sensitivity, always considering the victims and their families. It is essential to strike a balance between entertainment and responsible storytelling, ensuring that we do not glorify or romanticize the actions of these heinous criminals.

Copycat Crimes

In the dark and disturbing realm of crime, there exists a phenomenon that both fascinates and horrifies us: copycat crimes. These chilling acts of violence, explored in this subchapter, delve into the twisted psychology behind those who imitate the methods and motives of notorious serial killers.

Serial killers have long captivated the public's imagination, their heinous acts leaving a lasting mark on society. But what compels certain individuals to emulate these monsters, perpetuating a cycle of terror? To understand this perplexing phenomenon, we must first explore the intricate workings of the human mind.

The human psyche is a complex labyrinth, capable of both incredible compassion and unimaginable darkness. In the case of copycat crimes, it is this darkness that takes center stage. These individuals, often plagued by deep-seated psychological issues and a desire for notoriety, seek to emulate the deeds of their infamous predecessors.

Examining the psychology behind copycat crimes reveals a disturbing pattern. It is not uncommon for these individuals to idolize and idolize the original serial killer, obsessively studying their methods, motives, and even personal lives. This fixation gives birth to a dangerous fantasy, as they begin to see themselves as the inheritors of their idols' legacy.

Motives for copycat crimes vary, but some common themes emerge. Some seek recognition and a twisted form of fame, craving the media attention that comes with their crimes. Others aim to surpass their idols, driven by a desire to become the most notorious killer of their time. In these cases, the copycat crime acts as a macabre competition, a battle for supremacy in the annals of criminal history.

Understanding the psychology of copycat crimes is crucial for law enforcement agencies and criminal profilers alike. By recognizing the signs and patterns that drive these individuals, steps can be taken to prevent future acts of violence. Furthermore, studying these cases helps shed light on the minds of serial killers themselves, providing valuable insights into their motives and methods.

In this subchapter, we will delve into the chilling world of copycat crimes. Through the exploration of infamous cases and in-depth psychological analysis, we aim to unravel the intricate threads that connect these imitators to their murderous idols. Brace yourself for a journey into the dark recesses of the human mind, where the line between reality and fantasy becomes disturbingly blurred.

Criminal Profiling and Investigation Techniques

In the thrilling world of crime investigation, few aspects capture the imagination quite like the study of serial killers. These enigmatic individuals who commit multiple murders over an extended period of time have long fascinated both the general public and professionals in the field. Delving into the psychology and patterns of these killers, criminal profiling and investigation techniques have become invaluable tools in understanding and apprehending these dangerous criminals.

This subchapter aims to provide a comprehensive exploration into the world of criminal profiling and investigation techniques, with a specific focus on serial killers. By unraveling the psychology behind their crimes, we hope to shed light on the distinct characteristics and motives that drive these individuals to commit such heinous acts.

Criminal profiling, often referred to as behavioral profiling, is a technique that involves the careful analysis of crime scenes, victimology, and other evidence to develop a psychological profile of the offender. This profile aids investigators in narrowing down potential suspects and understanding their motivations, thus increasing the chances of apprehension.

One key aspect of criminal profiling in serial killer cases is the identification of common patterns and characteristics. By analyzing the modus operandi, signature, and victim selection, experts can identify recurring themes and behaviors that help create a profile of the killer. Understanding these patterns can assist investigators in predicting the offender's next move and preventing future crimes.

Furthermore, this subchapter will delve into the psychological theories that underpin the motivations of serial killers. From the power and control-seeking to the thrill of the kill, exploring these motives provides crucial insights into the minds of these perpetrators. By understanding their psychopathic tendencies, law enforcement officials can better anticipate their actions and devise strategies to bring them to justice.

Lastly, the subchapter will highlight the various investigative techniques employed in serial killer cases. It will explore the use of forensic evidence, including DNA analysis and crime scene reconstruction, as well as the utilization of advanced technology, such as geographic profiling and offender profiling software. These techniques have revolutionized the field of criminal investigation, aiding in the identification and capture of serial killers.

In conclusion, this subchapter on criminal profiling and investigation techniques offers a captivating insight into the world of serial killers. By examining their psychology, patterns, and motives, we hope to provide a comprehensive understanding of these individuals. Whether you are a crime enthusiast or a professional in the field, this subchapter will unveil the fascinating world of serial killers while offering valuable insights into their identification, apprehension, and the prevention of future crimes.

Chapter 9: The Role of Mental Health

Psychiatric Disorders and Serial Killers

Psychiatric disorders have long been a subject of fascination and study when it comes to understanding the mind of a serial killer. In this subchapter, we delve deep into the complex relationship between psychiatric disorders and the heinous acts committed by these individuals. By examining the psychology and patterns of serial killers, we aim to unravel the intricate web of mental afflictions that contribute to their murderous behaviors.

One of the most prominent psychiatric disorders associated with serial killers is psychopathy. Psychopaths are characterized by a lack of empathy, remorse, and a profound disregard for societal norms. Their ability to manipulate and charm others allows them to blend seamlessly into society, making it challenging to identify them as potential murderers. Within the realm of psychopathy, we explore subcategories such as primary and secondary psychopathy, shedding light on the varying degrees of this disorder and its impact on serial killings.

Another disorder frequently observed in serial killers is antisocial personality disorder (ASPD). Individuals with ASPD exhibit a persistent pattern of disregard for the rights of others, often engaging in impulsive and reckless behaviors. This disorder, coupled with a history of childhood abuse, neglect, or trauma, can create a fertile ground for the development of a serial killer. By understanding the intricacies of ASPD, we aim to uncover the factors that contribute to the transformation of troubled individuals into remorseless murderers.

Furthermore, our exploration delves into the realm of psychosis, such as schizophrenia or delusional disorder, and its connection to serial killings. While relatively rare among serial killers, psychosis can significantly impact their motivations and behaviors. We examine case studies where delusions or hallucinations have fueled a killer's deluded sense of purpose or driven them to commit unspeakable acts in pursuit of their distorted beliefs.

By examining the interplay between psychiatric disorders and serial killers, we hope to shed light on the complex nature of these crimes. Understanding the psychological underpinnings can aid law enforcement in profiling and apprehending these individuals, as well as assist mental health professionals in identifying potential warning signs and providing effective interventions. Moreover, this knowledge allows us to explore the fascinating question of whether these killers are victims of their own disorders or whether they possess agency over their actions.

Join us as we venture into the dark recesses of the human mind, unraveling the intricate connections between psychiatric disorders and the terrifying world of serial killers.

Psychiatric Evaluations and Treatments

Understanding the psychology behind the heinous crimes committed by serial killers is crucial in order to prevent, apprehend, and rehabilitate these individuals. In this subchapter, we delve into the world of psychiatric evaluations and treatments, shedding light on the methods used to analyze and treat the minds of these complex criminals.

Psychiatric evaluations play a pivotal role in unraveling the intricate workings of a serial killer's mind. These evaluations involve a comprehensive examination of the offender's mental health history, upbringing, and any potential psychological disorders. By delving deep into their past, psychiatrists can identify potential triggers, traumatic experiences, or underlying mental illnesses that may have contributed to their deviant behavior.

One common psychiatric evaluation tool used is the Diagnostic and Statistical Manual of Mental Disorders (DSM). This manual provides a standardized framework for classifying mental disorders, allowing professionals to diagnose and understand the psychological complexities of these criminals. By using the DSM, psychiatrists can identify disorders such as antisocial personality disorder, psychopathy, or sadism, which are often prevalent among serial killers.

Once a thorough evaluation is completed, a tailored treatment plan can be devised. Treatment in the case of serial killers often involves a multi-faceted approach, combining psychotherapy, medication, and behavioral modification techniques. Psychotherapy, such as cognitive-behavioral therapy, aims to identify and address the distorted thought patterns and behavioral triggers that contribute to their violent tendencies.

In some cases, medication may be prescribed to manage underlying mental disorders, such as depression or schizophrenia, which could be exacerbating their violent tendencies. However, it is important to note that medication alone is rarely sufficient in treating serial killers, and therapy is a fundamental component of their rehabilitation process.

Behavioral modification techniques, including anger management and impulse control strategies, are crucial in helping serial killers develop healthier coping mechanisms and self-regulation skills. By addressing the root causes of their violent behavior and teaching alternative ways of managing their emotions, these techniques aim to reduce the likelihood of recidivism.

Psychiatric evaluations and treatments are essential tools in unraveling the psychology behind serial killers. By understanding the complex interplay of factors that contribute to their crimes, professionals can work towards preventing future acts of violence, apprehending these offenders, and ultimately rehabilitating them. Through a combination of thorough evaluations, tailored treatment plans, and ongoing support, we can strive to unravel the enigma of the serial killer's mind and bring an end to their reign of terror.

The Debate on Nature vs. Nurture

The age-old debate on nature versus nurture has long fascinated experts in the field of psychology. When it comes to the perplexing and disturbing phenomenon of serial killers, this debate takes on a heightened significance. Are

these individuals born with a predisposition to commit such heinous acts, or are their actions shaped by environmental factors and upbringing? This subchapter delves into this contentious topic, exploring the various arguments and theories surrounding the nature versus nurture debate in the context of serial killers.
On one hand, proponents of the nature theory argue that certain individuals are genetically predisposed to violence and aggression. They argue that traits such as impulsivity, lack of empathy, and a predisposition towards violence can be inherited. Studies have pointed to the presence of certain genetic markers in serial killers, suggesting a biological basis for their behavior. Additionally, brain imaging studies have revealed abnormalities in the brains of some serial killers, supporting the idea that their violent tendencies may be hardwired.

On the other hand, advocates of the nurture theory emphasize the impact of environmental factors on the development of serial killers. Childhood abuse, neglect, and exposure to violence have all been identified as potential catalysts for the emergence of violent behavior later in life. The theory posits that early experiences shape an individual's worldview, leading to distorted perceptions and a propensity for violence. Moreover, the influence of socialization, peer relationships, and cultural factors cannot be overlooked when examining the psychology of serial killers.

It is important to note that the nature versus nurture debate is not a simple binary. In reality, the development of a serial killer is likely influenced by a complex interplay of both genetic and environmental factors. This interaction between nature and nurture is often referred to as gene-environment interaction. Some researchers argue that a genetic predisposition towards violence may require certain environmental triggers to manifest fully.

Understanding the nature versus nurture debate is crucial for comprehending the psychology and patterns of serial killers. By examining the interplay between an individual's genetic makeup and their environment, experts can gain insights into the motivations, triggers, and patterns of behavior displayed by these individuals. This knowledge is essential for developing effective prevention strategies, identifying potential warning signs, and ultimately, minimizing the occurrence of such horrific crimes.

In conclusion, the nature versus nurture debate is a fascinating and complex aspect of understanding serial killers. While both genetic and environmental factors undoubtedly play a role, the exact mechanisms that lead to the development of a serial killer remain elusive. By continuing to explore this debate, researchers and experts can uncover further insights into the psychology behind these crimes, ultimately contributing to a safer society.

Ethical Considerations in Treatment

In the study of serial killers, the exploration of their psychology and patterns is crucial to understanding the motives behind their heinous crimes. However, it is equally important to address the ethical considerations that arise when it comes to the treatment of these individuals. This subchapter delves into the complex ethical dilemmas faced by mental health professionals when attempting to understand and rehabilitate serial killers.

One of the primary ethical considerations in treating serial killers is the delicate balance between the rights of the individual and the safety of society. Mental health professionals must grapple with the question of whether it is possible to rehabilitate individuals who have committed multiple murders. Is it ethical to invest resources in their treatment, potentially at the expense of other individuals who may be in need? These questions raise profound ethical concerns that require careful thought and consideration.

Another ethical consideration is the potential exploitation of the knowledge gained from studying and treating serial killers. The information gathered through research and therapy sessions can be invaluable in terms of understanding the psychological underpinnings of their crimes. However, there is a fine line between using this knowledge for academic purposes and sensationalizing or glorifying their actions. It is crucial for researchers and writers to handle this information responsibly, ensuring that it is used for the betterment of society rather than for entertainment or exploitation.

Moreover, the issue of informed consent arises when working with serial killers. Given the nature of their crimes, it can be challenging to establish a genuine and voluntary consent for treatment. Mental health professionals must navigate this ethical quandary, ensuring that any therapy provided is both beneficial and respectful of the individual's autonomy.

Finally, the issue of confidentiality in treatment poses ethical challenges. Mental health professionals are bound by the duty to maintain patient confidentiality, but what happens when the individual poses a threat to society? Balancing the need for public safety with the ethical obligation to protect the privacy and trust of the patient can be a complex and emotionally charged task.

In conclusion, the study and treatment of serial killers demand careful ethical considerations. The rights of the individual, the safety of society, the responsible use of knowledge, informed consent, and confidentiality are all critical factors that mental health professionals must navigate. By approaching these ethical dilemmas with sensitivity and a commitment to the greater good, professionals can strive to unravel the psychology behind the crimes while upholding the principles of ethics and morality.

Chapter 10: Case Studies
Ted Bundy: Charming Manipulator
Subchapter: Ted Bundy: Charming Manipulator

Ted Bundy, one of the most infamous serial killers in history, was a master of manipulation. His charm and charisma masked a dark and twisted mind, allowing him to deceive and lure his victims with ease. In this subchapter, we delve into the enigmatic psyche of Ted Bundy, analyzing the psychological factors that contributed to his heinous crimes.

Bundy possessed an uncanny ability to present himself as an affable, charismatic individual, disarming those around him. His good looks, intelligence, and charming demeanor allowed him to gain the trust of his victims, making it easier for him to approach and overpower them. This subchapter explores the intricate web of manipulation Bundy wove, examining the methods he employed to exploit his victims' vulnerabilities.

One crucial aspect of Bundy's modus operandi was his capacity to adapt his appearance and behavior to suit the situation. By adopting different guises, he was able to blend seamlessly into various social circles, enabling him to approach potential victims undetected. We delve into the psychology behind this chameleon-like behavior, shedding light on how Bundy's ability to manipulate his outward persona facilitated his murderous activities.

Furthermore, this subchapter examines the role of Bundy's upbringing and personal experiences in shaping his malignant character. From an early age, Bundy displayed signs of deviant behavior, which escalated over time. We explore the key events and environmental factors that may have contributed to the formation of his psychopathic tendencies, shedding light on the inter-

play between nature and nurture in the creation of a serial killer.
As we unravel the psychology behind Bundy's crimes, we highlight the distinct characteristics and motives that set him apart from other serial killers. From his preference for attractive, young women to his propensity for necrophilia, Bundy's patterns of behavior reveal deep-seated psychological complexities. By understanding these intricacies, we gain insights into the inner workings of a charming manipulator, shedding light on the broader field of serial killer psychology.
In this subchapter, we aim to provide a comprehensive analysis of Ted Bundy as a charming manipulator. By examining the psychological factors that influenced his behavior and the patterns that emerged from his crimes, we deepen our understanding of the complex world of serial killers. Ultimately, this exploration serves as a cautionary tale, reminding us of the dangers that can lurk beneath the surface of even the most charming individuals.

Aileen Wuornos: Female Serial Killer

Throughout history, the world has been captivated by the chilling tales of serial killers, their motives, and the dark recesses of their minds. While the majority of notorious serial killers have been male, there have been a few cases that have shattered this stereotype. One such case is that of Aileen Wuornos, a female serial killer whose crimes shocked the nation and raised profound questions about the psychology behind her actions.

In this subchapter, we delve into the disturbing life and crimes of Aileen Wuornos, offering a glimpse into the mind of a female serial killer. Wuornos was a troubled individual, marked by a traumatic childhood and a series of unfortunate events that led her down a path of violence and murder.

Born in 1956, Wuornos had a tumultuous upbringing marred by abuse and neglect. Her troubled childhood, coupled with a string of failed relationships and prostitution, set the stage for the emergence of her dark side. Over a period of just one year, from 1989 to 1990, Wuornos embarked on a killing spree that claimed the lives of seven men. Her victims were often middle-aged, white males, and she targeted them while working as a prostitute.

Examining the psychology behind Wuornos' crimes reveals a complex interplay of factors that contributed to her violent behavior. Her troubled childhood, marked by physical and sexual abuse, undoubtedly played a significant role. The trauma she endured likely distorted her perception of relationships and fueled her rage towards men. Furthermore, her experiences in prostitution, where she faced exploitation and violence, may have further fueled her anger and desire for revenge.

Wuornos' case also raises intriguing questions about gender dynamics in serial killing. Traditionally, serial killers have been predominantly male, with distinct motivations such as sexual gratification or power. However, Wuornos' case challenges these notions, highlighting that women are also capable of committing heinous acts of violence. Understanding the unique motivations and psychological patterns of female serial killers is crucial for unraveling the complexities of criminal behavior.

In conclusion, the case of Aileen Wuornos offers a fascinating insight into the mind of a female serial killer. Her troubled past, coupled with the unique circumstances of her life, provided a breeding ground for her violent tendencies. By examining her psychology and the distinct patterns in her crimes, we gain a deeper understanding of the complex factors that contribute to serial killers' actions, regardless of gender. Ultimately, Wuornos' story serves as a haunting reminder that evil knows no gender boundaries and the human psyche can harbor unimaginable darkness.

Jeffrey Dahmer: The Cannibalistic Monster

In the dark realm of serial killers, few names strike fear and fascination as strongly as Jeffrey Dahmer. Known as the Milwaukee Cannibal, Dahmer's heinous crimes shocked the world and left an indelible mark on the annals of criminal history. Delving into the depths of his twisted psyche, this subchapter explores the horrifying journey of a man who descended into unimaginable depravity.

From an early age, Dahmer displayed disturbing signs of psychopathy, harboring macabre fantasies and exhibiting cruelty towards animals. However, it wasn't until his teenage years that his murderous tendencies truly manifested. Dahmer's first victim, Steven Hicks, would become the catalyst for a killing spree that would span over a decade.

Dahmer's modus operandi was chillingly distinct. He would lure vulnerable men, often from marginalized communities, to his lair under the pretext of companionship. Once trapped, he unleashed his sadistic desires upon them, engaging in acts of torture, necrophilia, and eventually cannibalism. The sheer brutality and methodical nature of his crimes revealed a deeply disturbed mind, driven by an insatiable urge for power and control.

Unraveling the psychology behind Dahmer's actions reveals a complex interplay of factors. Childhood neglect, a fractured family environment, and a sense of isolation played significant roles in shaping his distorted worldview. His desire for dominance and the need to possess his victims' bodies stemmed from a profound psychological void, a desperate attempt to fill the void within himself.

Dahmer's case raises critical questions about the nature of evil and the limits of human empathy. His ability to blend into society, appearing ordinary and unassuming, highlights the chilling reality that monsters can lurk among us, hidden behind a façade of normalcy. The patterns and characteristics of his crimes serve as a cautionary tale, urging society to remain vigilant and aware of the signs that may indicate the presence of a potential serial killer.

Ultimately, the case of Jeffrey Dahmer stands as a stark reminder of the depths to which human depravity can sink. It forces us to confront the uncomfortable truth that there may never be a definitive answer to why some individuals become serial killers. Nevertheless, by examining the psychology and patterns behind their crimes, we can hope to gain insights that may aid in the prevention and early detection of such horrors in the future.

As we explore the chilling details of Dahmer's monstrous acts, we must confront our darkest fears and strive to understand the mind of a serial killer, in the hope that by doing so, we can prevent the emergence of future monsters.

John Wayne Gacy: The Killer Clown

John Wayne Gacy, also known as the "Killer Clown," is one of the most notorious serial killers in American history. His heinous crimes shocked the nation and left a lasting impact on the field of criminal psychology. This subchapter delves deep into the twisted mind of Gacy, exploring the psychological factors and patterns that led him to commit his gruesome murders.

Gacy, a seemingly average and well-liked member of his community, harbored a dark secret. Behind the facade of a successful contractor and a volunteer clown at children's parties, he was a sadistic predator who targeted young boys. Gacy's ability to blend into society while leading a double life is a chilling characteristic shared by many serial killers.

To understand Gacy's psychology, it is crucial to examine his childhood and formative years. Raised in a strict and abusive household, Gacy experienced a turbulent relationship with his domineering father. These early experiences likely contributed to his development of a disturbed and twisted personality that later manifested in violent and predatory behavior.

Gacy's crimes were marked by a distinct pattern. He would lure his victims to his home under the pretense of offering them work or money. Once in his clutches, he would subject them to unimaginable acts of torture and sexual abuse before ultimately killing them. Gacy's ability to manipulate and control his victims highlights his sadistic nature and desire for power and dominance.

The killer clown persona that Gacy adopted reveals another layer of his psychological makeup. By dressing up as a clown, he could disarm his victims and gain their trust, exploiting his position of authority and familiarity. This macabre choice of disguise further illustrates the intricate and complex nature of Gacy's psychopathy.

The subchapter also explores the aftermath of Gacy's arrest and the subsequent investigation that uncovered the shocking extent of his crimes. The revelations surrounding his hidden crawl space, where the bodies of his victims were buried, horrified the nation and forever etched his name in the annals of criminal history.

John Wayne Gacy's case offers a chilling window into the mind of a serial killer. By examining his psychological makeup, patterns, and motives, we can gain valuable insights into the dark and twisted world of those who commit multiple murders over an extended period. This subchapter provides a comprehensive analysis of Gacy's crimes and their psychological underpinnings, shedding light on the complex and unsettling nature of serial killers.

Chapter 11: The Aftermath: Capturing and Understanding Serial Killers

In the dark and twisted world of serial killers, the pursuit and eventual capture of these heinous criminals is a crucial and captivating aspect. The tireless efforts of law enforcement agencies, forensic experts, and profilers make up the backbone of these investigations, often leading to the unraveling of the psychology behind these chilling crimes. This subchapter delves into the fascinating journey of investigating and capturing serial killers, shedding light on the tactics, challenges, and breakthroughs that occur during this harrowing process.

The investigation of serial killers involves a meticulous examination of crime scenes, analyzing evidence, and establishing patterns. Law enforcement agencies rely on cutting-edge forensic techniques to gather clues, such as DNA analysis, fingerprint identification, and ballistics. These investigations are often complex, spanning multiple jurisdictions, as the elusive nature of serial killers may lead them to commit crimes in various locations, making the task of connecting the dots even more challenging.

One of the key elements in the pursuit of serial killers is the involvement of profilers, experts in understanding the psychology and behavioral patterns of these criminals. Profilers meticulously study crime scenes, victimology, and the modus operandi of the killer to create a psychological profile. This profile assists investigators in narrowing down their search, identifying potential suspects, and developing strategies to apprehend the killer.

However, capturing a serial killer is no easy feat. These criminals are often cunning, evasive, and meticulous in covering their tracks. The investigation may span years, with countless dead ends and frustrating setbacks. Yet, the relentless determination of law enforcement personnel and their unwavering commitment to justice often leads to breakthroughs that ultimately bring these monsters to justice.

This subchapter also explores the psychological toll that investigating serial killers can have on those involved. The intense exposure to gruesome crimes and the constant pursuit of an elusive killer can take a significant toll on the mental well-being of investigators. It is crucial to understand the importance of providing support and counseling to those immersed in these investigations to ensure their own mental health and well-being.

The investigation and capture of serial killers is a dark and intricate dance between the criminal and those determined to bring them to justice. It is a testament to human resilience, the power of forensic science, and the unwavering commitment of law enforcement agencies. By unraveling the psychology and patterns behind these crimes, we gain insight into the minds of these disturbed individuals, contributing to the prevention and understanding of such atrocities in the future.

Trial and Legal Consequences

Once a serial killer is apprehended, the legal process begins, unraveling the twisted web of their crimes. This subchapter delves into the crucial phase of bringing these individuals to justice and explores the legal consequences they face for their heinous actions.

The trial of a serial killer is a complex affair, often spanning months or even years. The prosecution meticulously presents its case, relying on a combination of forensic evidence, witness testimonies, and expert analysis to establish guilt beyond a reasonable doubt. The defense, on the other hand, seeks to cast doubt on the evidence and challenge the prosecution's narrative.

Given the high-profile nature of these cases, they often attract intense media scrutiny. The courtroom becomes a stage where the public awaits justice, seeking answers and closure for the victims and their families. The trial becomes a battle not only for legal victory but also for the hearts and minds of the jury and the wider public.

During the trial, the prosecution attempts to shed light on the psychology of the serial killer. Expert witnesses, such as forensic psychologists and profilers, provide invaluable insights into the mind of the perpetrator. They analyze the motives, patterns, and characteristics of the killer, helping the jury understand the psychology behind the crimes committed.

While the ultimate goal of the trial is to secure a conviction, the legal consequences vary depending on the jurisdiction. In some countries, serial killers may face the death penalty, while in others, life imprisonment without the possibility of parole may be the harshest sentence. The judge's decision takes into account factors such as the severity of the crimes, the killer's level of premeditation, and any mitigating or aggravating circumstances.

Furthermore, the trial provides an opportunity for the victims' families to share their impact statements, expressing the profound emotional, psychological, and physical toll the crimes have had on their lives. These statements humanize the victims, ensuring that their voices are heard and reminding the court of the devastating consequences of the killer's actions.

Ultimately, the trial and its legal consequences mark the end of the road for the serial killer. It is a moment when society seeks closure, and justice is served. This subchapter offers a detailed exploration of this critical phase, shedding light on the inner workings of the legal system and the consequences these twisted individuals face for their crimes.

Rehabilitation and Recidivism

In the realm of criminal psychology, one of the most perplexing phenomena to understand is the concept of rehabilitation and recidivism among serial killers. The desire to comprehend what drives these individuals to commit multiple murders over a period of time, often with distinct characteristics or motives, is crucial in order to prevent future atrocities and protect society.

Rehabilitation, in its essence, refers to the process of restoring an individual to a state of normalcy, both physically and mentally, after being involved in criminal activities. However, when it comes to serial killers, the effectiveness of rehabilitation programs becomes a topic of intense debate. Many argue that the deep-rooted psychological issues and ingrained patterns of violence exhibited by these individuals make rehabilitation an arduous task.

Understanding the psychology behind serial killers is paramount in crafting effective rehabilitation programs. It is widely acknowledged that these individuals often display psychopathic or sociopathic traits, which hinder their ability to experience remorse or empathy. Moreover, their twisted fantasies and compulsions drive them to commit heinous acts repeatedly, making it challenging to address the underlying causes of their behavior.

Recidivism, or the tendency of a convicted criminal to reoffend, is a critical concern in the context of serial killers. The recidivism rates among this group are alarmingly high, raising questions about the effectiveness of rehabilitation efforts. While some argue that certain individuals may be rehabilitated and reintegrated into society successfully, others maintain that the ingrained nature of their psychopathy makes recidivism an inevitable outcome.

To tackle this complex issue, it is crucial to adopt a multidimensional approach. Rehabilitation programs should focus not only on therapy and counseling but also on addressing the root causes of the individual's violent tendencies. This may involve exploring childhood trauma, dysfunctional family dynamics, or any other factors that may have contributed to the development of their psychopathy.

Furthermore, post-release monitoring and support systems play a pivotal role in preventing recidivism among serial killers. Close supervision, ongoing therapy, and community reintegration programs can help these individuals adjust to a life without violence and provide them with the necessary tools to resist their dark impulses.

In conclusion, the topic of rehabilitation and recidivism among serial killers is a complex and challenging one. While the effectiveness of rehabilitation programs remains a subject of debate, it is imperative that society continues to explore and develop strategies to understand the psychology behind these individuals. By delving into the depths of their minds, we can hope to unravel the intricacies of their crimes and work towards preventing future tragedies.

Lessons Learned and Preventive Measures

In delving into the dark and complex world of serial killers, it becomes crucial to extract valuable lessons from their heinous crimes. By understanding the psychology and patterns behind these individuals, we can gain insights that may help prevent future tragedies. This chapter aims to explore key lessons learned from studying serial killers and propose preventive measures to safeguard society.

One of the most significant lessons is the recognition that many serial killers exhibit distinct characteristics and motives. By identifying these traits, law enforcement agencies and mental health professionals can potentially identify and intervene before these individuals escalate to violence. Behavioral profiling and psychological assessments can be invaluable tools in identifying potential serial killers and preventing them from fulfilling their murderous desires.

Another crucial lesson is the importance of early intervention and support for individuals who display troubling behaviors or have a history of violence. Often, serial killers exhibit warning signs during their childhood or adolescence, such as cruelty to animals, bedwetting, or arson. By providing timely and comprehensive mental health services, we can address the underlying issues that contribute to their violent tendencies.

Furthermore, effective communication and collaboration between law enforcement agencies, mental health professionals, and communities are vital preventive measures. Establishing multidisciplinary task forces that bring together experts from various fields can enhance the ability to identify and apprehend potential serial killers. Additionally, fostering a culture that encourages community members to report suspicious activities or behaviors without fear of retribution can be instrumental in preventing future crimes.

Education and awareness play a pivotal role in preventing serial killings. By disseminating information about the characteristics and patterns of these criminals, as well as the warning signs that may precede their actions, individuals can be better equipped to identify potential threats. This knowledge can empower people to take action and report suspicious activities promptly.

Lastly, investing in research and understanding the complex psychology behind serial killers is crucial for developing effective preventive measures. By continuously studying and analyzing these individuals, we can refine our understanding of their motivations, triggers, and patterns. This knowledge can inform the development of targeted intervention programs and strategies that can help identify and rehabilitate individuals at risk of becoming serial killers.

In conclusion, the study of serial killers provides invaluable insights into their psychology and patterns. By applying the lessons learned and implementing preventive measures, we can strive to protect society from these individuals and prevent the loss of innocent lives. It is through a multidisciplinary approach, early intervention, education, and collaboration that we can hope to unravel the mysteries behind these crimes and work towards a safer future.

Chapter 12: The Future of Serial Killers

Technological Advancements and Serial Killers

In the ever-evolving world of technology, it is no surprise that advancements have had a profound impact on various aspects of our lives. From communication to transportation, technology has transformed the way we live and interact with one another. This subchapter aims to explore the intriguing intersection between technological advancements and the psychology of serial killers.

Serial killers have long been subjects of fascination for both the general public and professionals within the field of criminology. These individuals commit multiple murders over a period of time, often displaying distinct characteristics or motives. With the advent of technology, the study of serial killers has taken on a whole new dimension, shedding light on their behavior, motives, and patterns.

One of the most significant ways in which technology has influenced the study of serial killers is through the advancement of forensic science. DNA analysis, for instance, has revolutionized criminal investigations, allowing law enforcement to link crimes to specific individuals with unprecedented accuracy. This breakthrough has not only helped solve cold cases but has also contributed to the identification and apprehension of serial killers who may have otherwise remained undetected.

Moreover, the rise of the internet and social media has provided a platform for the dissemination of information related to serial killers. Online communities dedicated to discussing and analyzing the psychology behind their crimes have emerged, allowing experts and enthusiasts to share insights and theories. This virtual space has facilitated a greater understanding of the mindsets and motives of these dangerous individuals.

However, it is important to note that technology has also presented challenges in combating serial killers. The anonymity and ease of communication afforded by the internet have enabled potential offenders to connect with like-minded individuals and even exchange tips on evading law enforcement. The digital age has given rise to a new breed of "cyber killers," who utilize technology to exploit and harm their victims.

In conclusion, technological advancements have had a profound impact on the study of serial killers. From the advancements in forensic science, aiding in identification and apprehension, to the rise of online communities, allowing for a deeper understanding of the psychology behind their crimes, technology has opened up new avenues for research. However, it also poses challenges, as criminals adapt to and exploit the very technology that could be used against them. As technology continues to evolve, it is crucial for law enforcement and experts in the field to stay abreast of these advancements to effectively combat the dark world of serial killers.

Online Presence and Digital Criminology

In the digital age, the online presence of individuals has become an integral part of our lives. As our lives intertwine with the virtual world, so do the lives of criminals, including serial killers. The study of online presence in the context of digital criminology offers unique insights into the psychology and patterns of these individuals who commit multiple murders over a period of time, often with distinct characteristics or motives.

The internet has provided serial killers with a new platform to showcase their deviant behavior and interact with potential victims. Social media platforms, chat rooms, and online forums have become breeding grounds for criminal activities. Understanding the online presence of serial killers is crucial for law enforcement agencies and researchers to identify potential threats and prevent future crimes.

One aspect of online presence that digital criminology focuses on is the patterns and behaviors exhibited by serial killers in their online activities. By analyzing their online interactions, law enforcement professionals can gain valuable insights into their psychological makeup, motives, and potential targets. For example, some serial killers may use online platforms to engage in "trolling" behavior, seeking attention or validation for their actions. Others may join specific interest groups or forums related to their motives, such as discussions on violence, sadism, or specific victim types.

Moreover, digital footprints left by serial killers can provide critical evidence in criminal investigations. Law enforcement agencies can track their online activities, such as email communications, social media posts, or even online purchases, to establish connections, timelines, and potential accomplices. Digital criminology plays a pivotal role in analyzing these digital footprints, aiding investigators in piecing together the puzzle of a serial killer's actions.

However, the online presence of serial killers also poses challenges to law enforcement and the general public. These individuals often employ tactics to remain anonymous or mislead investigators, creating a digital smokescreen that can be difficult to penetrate. Cybersecurity measures, such as encryption or anonymizing tools, can make it challenging to track their online activities. Therefore, staying one step ahead in the digital realm is crucial for law enforcement agencies to effectively combat the menace of serial killers.

In conclusion, the study of online presence and digital criminology offers unique insights into the psychology and patterns of serial killers. By understanding their online interactions, behaviors, and digital footprints, law enforcement agencies can identify potential threats, gather crucial evidence, and prevent future crimes. However, the ever-evolving digital landscape presents challenges that must be overcome to effectively combat the crimes committed by these individuals. The exploration of online presence and digital criminology is essential for unraveling the psychology behind the crimes of serial killers and ensuring the safety of society.

Emerging Trends and Changing Patterns

In the ever-evolving world of criminal psychology, it is crucial to stay abreast of the emerging trends and changing patterns within the realm of serial killers. Understanding the psychology and patterns of individuals who commit multiple murders over a period of time, often with distinct characteristics or motives, is imperative for both law enforcement professionals and those with a keen interest in the dark realm of crime.

One of the most prominent emerging trends in the study of serial killers is the shift towards a more holistic approach. Traditionally, the focus has been on individual cases and the specific modus operandi of each killer. However, contemporary research is now delving deeper into the underlying factors that contribute to the development of a serial killer. This includes exploring childhood trauma, psychological disorders, and socio-environmental influences that may shape the deviant behavior.

Moreover, technological advancements have significantly impacted the methods and patterns of serial killers. The rise of the digital age has provided a new platform for potential offenders to interact, share information, and even find inspiration from their peers. Online communities, often referred to as "murderabilia" or "killer fandom," have emerged, providing a chilling insight into the twisted minds of these individuals. Such platforms not only facilitate the exchange of ideas but also act as virtual echo chambers, potentially fueling the escalation of violent tendencies.

The changing patterns of serial killers also extend to their motives and victim selection. While some killers may exhibit clear patterns in terms of victim type or geographical location, others have become more adept at evading detection by diversifying their targets. This unpredictability has made it increasingly challenging for law enforcement agencies to effectively profile and apprehend these dangerous individuals.

Furthermore, the rise of female serial killers has been a notable shift in recent years. Historically, the majority of serial killers have been male, but the emergence of female offenders has presented a new dimension to the study of serial murder. Understanding the distinctive motives, methods, and psychological factors that drive female serial killers is crucial for developing effective prevention strategies and enhancing public safety.

In conclusion, the subchapter on "Emerging Trends and Changing Patterns" serves as an essential guide for anyone interested in the psychology and patterns of serial killers. By exploring the holistic approach, technological influences, evolving motives, and the emergence of female offenders, readers gain a comprehensive understanding of the complexities surrounding these heinous crimes. This knowledge not only helps law enforcement professionals in their investigations but also raises awareness among the general public, contributing to a safer society.

Predictive Analysis and Profiling Advances

In recent years, the field of criminal psychology has witnessed significant advancements in the application of predictive analysis and profiling techniques to understand the minds of serial killers. This subchapter delves into the fascinating developments that have revolutionized our understanding of the psychology and patterns of these individuals who commit multiple murders over a period of time, often with distinct characteristics or motives.

Predictive analysis, also known as behavioral profiling, involves the use of data analysis and statistical modeling to identify patterns and trends in a serial killer's behavior, allowing investigators to anticipate their next move. By examining the crime scenes, victimology, and other pertinent details, experts can draw inferences about the killer's modus operandi, signature, and potential target preferences. This predictive approach has been instrumental in narrowing down suspects and prioritizing investigative efforts, leading to the capture of numerous notorious serial killers.

One notable advance in predictive analysis is the incorporation of geospatial profiling. By analyzing the spatial patterns of a serial killer's crimes, experts can create a map that highlights the areas most likely to be targeted in the future. This technique has proven highly effective in predicting the offender's base of operations, aiding law enforcement agencies in allocating resources and conducting targeted surveillance.

Furthermore, advancements in technology have paved the way for the development of sophisticated psychological profiling tools. These tools leverage machine learning algorithms and artificial intelligence to analyze vast amounts of data, including crime scene details, witness statements, and the killer's background information. By identifying patterns and correlations that may elude human analysts, these tools provide valuable insights into the psychological makeup and motivations of serial killers.

Additionally, research in the field of neuroscience has contributed to our understanding of the underlying biological factors that may predispose individuals to become serial killers. Advanced brain imaging techniques have revealed structural and functional abnormalities in certain regions of the brains of serial killers, shedding light on the potential neurological basis for their violent tendencies.

As our knowledge of predictive analysis and profiling advances, so does our ability to prevent and solve crimes committed by serial killers. By harnessing the power of data, technology, and neuroscience, we gain a deeper understanding of the intricate workings of these criminal minds. This subchapter serves as a comprehensive exploration of the cutting-edge techniques and breakthroughs that have unraveled the psychology behind serial killers, empowering law enforcement agencies and criminal psychologists in their tireless pursuit of justice.

Chapter 13: Conclusion: Unmasking the Dark Minds

Recap of Key Findings

Throughout this book, "Inside the Mind of a Serial Killer: Unraveling the Psychology Behind the Crimes," we have delved into the disturbing world of serial killers – individuals who commit multiple murders over a period of time, often with distinct characteristics or motives. The study of their psychology and patterns has provided valuable insights into their twisted minds, helping us to better understand the motivations behind their heinous acts.

One key finding that emerges from our exploration is that serial killers are not a homogeneous group. They come from different backgrounds, exhibit diverse personalities, and vary in their methods of operation. However, several common psychological traits have been identified among them. Many serial killers display a lack of empathy and an inability to form genuine emotional connections with others. This emotional detachment allows them to view their victims as objects rather than individuals with lives and families.

Another important finding is that childhood experiences often play a significant role in shaping the minds of serial killers. Many of them have suffered from abuse, neglect, or witnessed violence during their formative years. These traumatic events can create a breeding ground for the development of psychopathic tendencies, as the individual's capacity for empathy is stunted, and they may resort to violence as a means of control or coping mechanism.

Furthermore, research indicates that serial killers often display patterns in their behavior, known as modus operandi and signature. Modus operandi refers to the specific techniques or methods used to commit the crimes, while the signature represents the unique aspects of the crime that hold personal significance for the killer. By studying these patterns, investigators can gain valuable insights into the mind of the perpetrator and potentially link cases that may be connected.

It is also important to note that while the majority of serial killers are male, there have been significant cases involving female serial killers as well. The motives and methods employed by female serial killers may differ from their male counterparts, but the underlying psychological factors, such as a desire for power or control, remain consistent.

In conclusion, our exploration into the psychology and patterns of serial killers has revealed several key findings. These individuals often possess a lack of empathy, are shaped by traumatic childhood experiences, and display distinct patterns in their behavior. By understanding these traits and delving into the minds of serial killers, we can continue to advance our knowledge of criminology and hopefully prevent future tragedies.

Implications for Law Enforcement and Mental Health Professionals

Understanding the psychology behind the crimes of serial killers is crucial for both law enforcement and mental health professionals. As these individuals commit multiple murders over a period of time, often with distinct characteristics or motives, it becomes imperative to delve into their minds to develop strategies for prevention, detection, and intervention.

Law enforcement agencies play a critical role in apprehending serial killers and bringing them to justice. By grasping the psychological patterns and motives of these criminals, investigators can develop profiles that aid in narrowing down potential suspects. This allows for a more targeted and efficient investigation, saving valuable time and resources. Additionally, knowledge of the psychology behind these crimes can help law enforcement agencies identify potential hotspots or vulnerable populations that may be at higher risk, enabling them to allocate resources accordingly.

Furthermore, understanding the psychology of serial killers can assist mental health professionals in developing comprehensive prevention and intervention strategies. By identifying common traits, early warning signs, and risk factors associated with serial killers, mental health practitioners can work towards early identification and intervention. This may involve conducting thorough assessments of individuals displaying concerning behaviors, providing appropriate support and treatment, and collaborating with law enforcement agencies to mitigate potential risks.

In addition to prevention and intervention efforts, mental health professionals can also contribute to the rehabilitation and reintegration of individuals who have committed multiple murders. By gaining insight into the psychological factors that drove these individuals to commit such heinous acts, mental health professionals can develop tailored treatment plans that address the underlying issues. This can include therapy, counseling, and other evidence-based interventions aimed at reducing the risk of reoffending.

Ultimately, the implications for law enforcement and mental health professionals in unraveling the psychology behind serial killers are far-reaching. By utilizing this knowledge, these professionals can work together to prevent future crimes, protect vulnerable populations, and provide a path towards rehabilitation for those who have already committed such horrific acts. It is through this collaborative effort that society can strive towards a safer and more compassionate future.

The Ongoing Battle Against Serial Killers

When it comes to the dark and twisted realm of serial killers, a battle has been raging for decades. Law enforcement agencies, psychologists, and criminologists have tirelessly worked to unravel the psychology behind these heinous crimes. In the book "Inside the Mind of a Serial Killer: Unraveling the Psychology Behind the Crimes," we delve deep into the minds of these monsters, exploring their motives, patterns, and the ongoing fight to bring them to justice.

Serial killers have been a subject of fascination and horror for the public, but for those involved in the field of crime, they are the ultimate puzzle to solve. The book explores the intricate psychology behind these cold-blooded killers, examining their motives, triggers, and the distinct characteristics that set them apart from other criminals. By understanding the inner workings of their minds, law enforcement agencies can better equip themselves to catch these predators before they strike again.

One of the key aspects explored in this subchapter is the patterns that serial killers often exhibit. Through extensive research and case studies, we uncover the commonalities among these murderers, from their choice of victims to their methods of operation. By recognizing these patterns, investigators can create profiles that aid in identifying and apprehending these killers more efficiently.

However, the battle against serial killers is far from over. With advancements in forensic science and the advent of technology, law enforcement agencies have gained valuable tools in their pursuit of justice. The book discusses the role of DNA analysis, criminal profiling, and the use of databases to link unsolved cases, shedding light on the progress made in recent years.

Furthermore, the book addresses the challenges faced by investigators in their quest to apprehend these elusive criminals. Serial killers are often highly intelligent and meticulous, leaving little evidence behind. The cat-and-mouse game between law enforcement and these killers is examined, highlighting the painstaking efforts made by investigators to bring closure to the victims' families.

"The Ongoing Battle Against Serial Killers" serves as a testament to the tireless efforts of those dedicated to understanding and combating these monsters. It offers a glimpse into the fascinating world of criminal psychology, appealing to true crime enthusiasts and those seeking a deeper understanding of the human psyche. By unraveling the mysteries behind these heinous crimes, we inch closer to preventing future atrocities and ensuring that justice is served.

Final Thoughts and Reflections

As we reach the conclusion of this compelling journey into the twisted minds of serial killers, it is essential to reflect upon the key insights and revelations that have been uncovered. Throughout the book, "Inside the Mind of a Serial Killer: Unraveling the Psychology Behind the Crimes," we have delved deep into the darkest corners of human psychology, attempting to understand the motivations, patterns, and characteristics that drive these individuals to commit multiple murders over an extended period.

One of the most poignant realizations is that serial killers are not simply monsters, but complex human beings with intricate psychological profiles. The diverse range of motives and characteristics displayed by these individuals underscores the importance of comprehending the unique circumstances that shape their actions. From the power-hungry lust for dominance to the deeply rooted trauma and psychological disorders, we have witnessed the multifaceted nature of these killers.

Moreover, our exploration has revealed the significance of early life experiences and environmental factors in the development of a potential serial killer. Childhood abuse, neglect, and exposure to violence can all contribute to the formation of a disturbed psyche, one that may eventually manifest itself through acts of extreme violence. Understanding these factors is crucial in developing effective preventative measures and early intervention strategies.

The patterns and rituals that emerge from the examination of serial killers' crimes have also been a critical focus of this book. From the choice of victims to the methods of killing, these patterns offer valuable insights into the mind of the killer. By understanding these patterns, law enforcement agencies and profilers can enhance their ability to identify, track, and apprehend these dangerous individuals.

As we conclude our exploration, it is important to remember the victims and their families, whose lives have been irreversibly shattered by these heinous acts. By shedding light on the psychology behind serial killers, we hope to contribute to society's understanding and prevention of such crimes.

In closing, "Inside the Mind of a Serial Killer: Unraveling the Psychology Behind the Crimes" has provided a comprehensive examination of the psychological underpinnings of these disturbing individuals. By studying the motives, characteristics, and patterns of serial killers, we can work towards developing strategies that may ultimately save lives and protect our communities from future atrocities. May this book serve as a testament to the resilience of the human spirit and as a reminder of the importance of continued research and vigilance in combating these horrific crimes.

www.ingramcontent.com/pod-product-compliance
Lightning Source LLC
Chambersburg PA
CBHW050852260726
48660CB00006B/2593
9798866307821